Guided Reading Journal

for

Crooked Letter, Crooked Letter

by Tom Franklin

This book belongs to

....

Harald Weisshaar

Guided Reading Journal

Crooked Letter, Crooked Letter

by Tom Franklin

Ernst Klett Sprachen
Stuttgart

1. Auflage 1 ⁵ ⁴ ³ ² ¹ | 2022 21 20 19 18

alle Zitate aus *Crooked Letter, Crooked Letter* by Tom Franklin
© Ernst Klett Sprachen GmbH, Rotebühlstraße 77, 70178 Stuttgart 2016
mit freundlicher Genehmigung von Pan, an imprint of Pan Macmillan, GB

© Ernst Klett Sprachen GmbH, Rotebühlstraße 77, 70178 Stuttgart 2018
Alle Rechte vorbehalten.
www.klett-sprachen.de

Autor: Prof. Harald Weisshaar

Redaktion: Debby Böhm
Layoutkonzeption: Greta Gröttrup
Illustrationen: Sven Palmowski, Barcelona
Icons: 0melapics / Freepik, Layerace / Freepik
Ton: Joschi Kauffmann, Stuttgart
Sprecher: Jonathan Tilley, Stuttgart
Gestaltung und Satz: Joachim Schrimm, bostext OHG, Friolzheim
Umschlaggestaltung: Greta Gröttrup
Titelbild: fotolia.com (forcdan), New York, Shutterstock (Sabphoto), New York
Druck und Bindung: Medienhaus Plump GmbH, Rheinbreitbach

Printed in Germany

ISBN 978-3-12-579904-2

9 783125 799042

Contents

Preface 6

1   Reading Guide 10
1.1   Chapter 1   11
1.2   Chapter 2   19
1.3   Chapter 3   28
1.4   Chapter 4   33
1.5   Chapter 5   38
1.6   Chapter 6   45
1.7   Chapter 7   51
1.8   Chapter 8   59
1.9   Chapter 9   64
1.10 Chapter 10   71
1.11 Chapter 11   76
1.12 Chapter 12   80
1.13 Chapter 13   85
1.14 Chapter 14   89
1.15 Chapter 15   93
1.16 Chapter 16   98
1.17 Chapter 17   101
1.18 Chapter 18   105
1.19 Chapter 19   108
1.20 In a nutshell   111

2.   Characters 118
2.1   Characterization   118
2.2   Useful vocab   118
2.3   Character profiles:
      Larry   122
      Silas   124
      Wallace   126
2.4   Relationships   128

3.   Clues 130

4   Classroom Material 140
4.1   The Language of the South   141
4.2   Fitting in   143
4.3   Definitions   146
4.4   Larry's isolation   149
4.5   A reading challenge   151
4.6   Turning points   153
4.7   Storytelling –
      Larry and his father   156
4.8   Guilt and redemption   158
4.9   Chronology of events   160

5   Digging Deeper 162

6   Your Notes 180

7   Solutions of sorts 186

Credits   200

Preface

Dear student,

what you're looking at right now is a *Guided Reading Journal* that's waiting to be filled by you. It is designed to help you read (and understand) *Crooked Letter, Crooked Letter* by Tom Franklin. There are a number of different features: sometimes, they will give you advice on what to look out for **while** reading, other times they will ask you to take notes on certain important issues **after** you've read a chapter. The important thing is that there's lots of space for your own thoughts and feelings, as you would expect in a reading log, except we're nudging you in the direction that we think you'll find helpful for your exam preparation. We strongly believe that often there is no right or wrong in understanding literature – but rather that there are good ways of arguing your point and less successful ways. This reading log is supposed to help you to argue well – even if you end up disagreeing with other people. You'll improve your vocabulary and language on the go as it were and save time when revising for your final exam (or *Abitur*).

Seeing as 7 is a lucky number, there are 7 sections in the book. The main part of this book is made up of Section 1, the **Reading Guide**. This takes you through the novel chapter by chapter with the following standard features:
a) The story (symbols, chapter summary, characters, setting)
b) Quotes (understanding and finding relevant quotes)
c) Vocabulary & language, and a
d) Sneak preview to the next chapter in the novel.

Section 2 is devoted to **characters** while section 3 helps you to keep track of the **clues** concerning the crimes. These will also help you keep track of the chronology of events – which can be tricky at times as the story jumps between times and perspectives. Section 4 contains some of the **worksheets** your teacher might also use in class. We thought that these would help you while reading, so we have included them here. Section 5 is called '**Digging Deeper**' and helps you do just that: where suitable we've added suggestions on how you can get your teeth even further into the novel. Section 6 is pure space for your very **own notes, pictures and other materials** and Section 7 contains some of the **solutions**. Seeing as this is your reading experience, we cannot anticipate your responses to many of the tasks, so these have not been included.

As a special feature, we have added **audio files** and **pictures** to make your reading experience multi-dimensional. All these extras can be accessed via the Augmented App.

Last but foremost: this is **your** reading log! It is waiting for you to fill it with your ideas, notes, feelings, thoughts, pictures, play-lists , doodles and whatever else pops into your mind.

Enjoy!

Your *Crooked Letter, Crooked Letter* team

Online material

There's a lot of additional material available for this book.
If you have a mobile phone or a tablet, you can download the
Klett Augmented App to access all the files and links.
Scan the pages with the Augmented Icon using the camera on your mobile phone
or tablet. Then download the files for this chapter.

 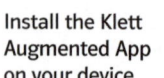

Install the Klett
Augmented App
on your device …

Start picture
recognition and scan
the first page of
a section or the page
with this icon:

Download files and
use them straight away
or save them for later.
You will need them
when you see this
reminder:

Should you not have access to a mobile device, you can still get to the material via
www.klett-sprachen.de.
Just enter the code **thh4egd** into the search field.

Symbols

A fairly obvious one: get scribbling!

This means you need to scan the page with the **Augmented App** to access all the additional files relevant for this chapter.

This is a reminder that there is **extra material**. You can find it in your app, if you've scanned the relevant page and have saved the files.

Get creative: **find or create** material and stick or draw it in the space provided.

Something to **listen** to.

This is where **your** feelings, opinions, ideas go.

Relevant for the **Abitur exam** (in terms of content and complexity).

This is information that relates to **characters** – for you to find quickly when revising.

This one points to **clues** that might be relevant to keep track of the story.

This points you to a different **section** of the book.

References to the novel (*Klett English Edition*) are made as follows:
page line ⇨ **38** 17–19 = **page 38,** lines 17–19.

Before you start reading

What **atmosphere** is conveyed on the cover?

What are the **central elements**?

What do you **expect** from this novel? What do you think it's about?

A Reading Challenge

This book really is a challenge. Find out how you can best tackle it.

Go to pages 151–152 in Section 4. It makes sense to look at these two pages before you start reading the novel!

Sneak Preview

A missing girl, a monster, an idyllic farm with chickens and then … Bang!

Focus is on: ☐ Larry ☐ Silas ☐ both

1.1   Chapter One – 8 pages

The story

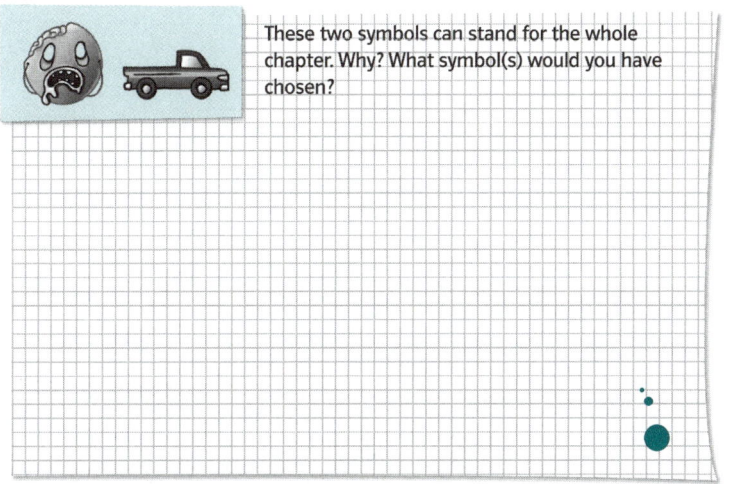

These two symbols can stand for the whole chapter. Why? What symbol(s) would you have chosen?

Here is a short **chapter summary**. Circle the correct options so you end up with a coherent version of what happens in the first chapter.

Summary

We get to know **Larry Ott / Mississippi / Tom Franklin**. Throughout the first chapter, there are many references and clues that hint at his being **lonely / 'unusual' / resigned**. Eventually, we find out that Larry, who is **41 / 32 / 46** years of age and **divorced / single / married**, has been **praised / ostracized / forgotten** by the local community ever since a **snake / letterbox / girl** he took **down / home / on a date** when he was **12 / a teenager / drunk** disappeared. Now, another girl has **fallen pregnant / gone missing / turned wild**. At the end of the chapter, Larry is **killed / shot / scared off** by a man wearing Larry's **leather boots / tool belt / zombie mask**.

1. Reading Guide

 What do you learn about the **central character**?

 Collect information on characters and useful vocab in Section 2 (p. 121 ff.).

Larry Ott

What would you like to find out about him?

Setting

What effect does the description of the landscape / the town have on you?
What pictures are evoked in your mind? Find pictures in magazines / on the
internet and stick them here or jot down some relevant adjectives.

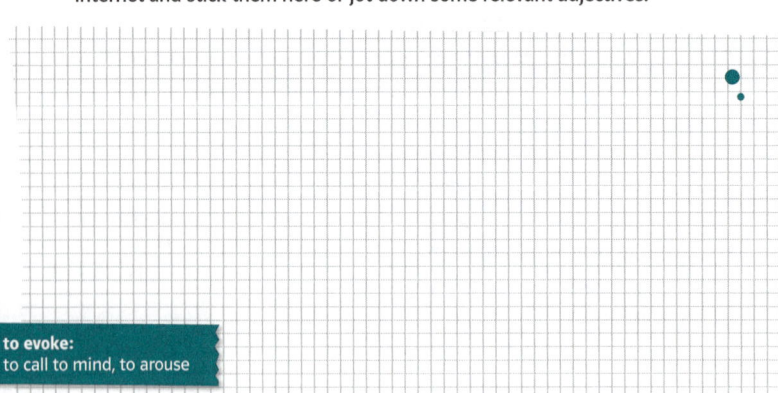

to evoke:
to call to mind, to arouse

Vocab & Language

➢ Here are **ten important words** from these pages.
  What do they mean? Translate or explain.

abduct	
bobwire	
bumblebee	
clutch	
croak	
curator	
deny	
gaze	
muddy	
reverse	

➢ What do you think about the book so far? Choose **three** of the following
  adjectives. Be prepared to explain your choice. Use two different colors:
  one for 'positive', one for 'negative' adjectives.

fast-paced   interesting   lackluster

        exciting   predictable   motivating

   difficult   promising   thrilling
                                                    cool

        boring   unusual
                breathtaking

   confusing   surprising
                    dull

1. Reading Guide

➢ Note down expressions or phrases from this chapter that you like and might want to recycle in your own writing:

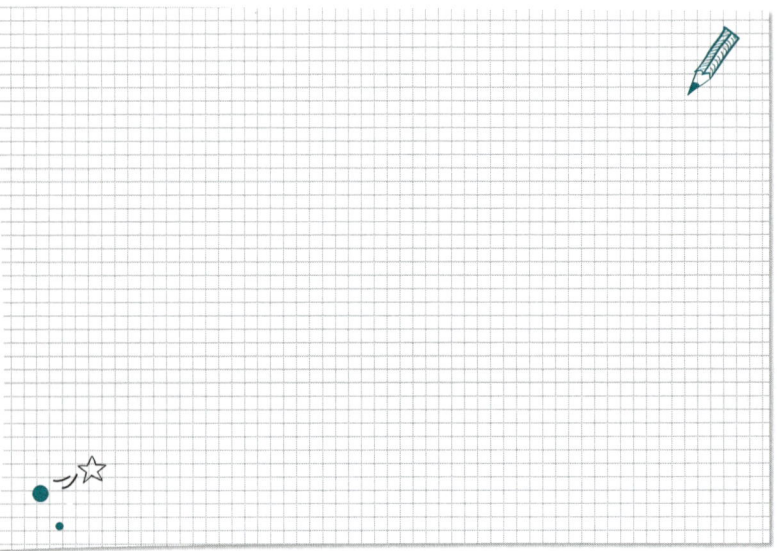

➢ Write down **three words** from this chapter that

are completely irrelevant to you:	you **like the sound of**:	you'd like to remember:
►	►	►
►	►	►
►	►	►

....

Talk about it! Useful words to describe this chapter:

| suspense | mystery | building tension | cliffhanger |

How do you expect the story to go on?

Have you found any **clue** or any conflict that you think will be further developed?

Quotes

It possibly makes sense to underline these quotes in your novel.

As you read the novel, you will come across many important passages.

This 'Quotes'-section can help you to find key sentences from the novel again once you're through with the book.

For the first few chapters, we will print three or four of the most central quotes in this section. You can note down what *you* think their relevance is or what context they appear in. A suggestion is provided via the Augmented App.

Other important sentences are indicated by giving you the page and the line references (e.g. **17** 6–9 = page 17, lines 6–9).

Later on, we will ask *you* to decide which sentences *you* find important or meaningful, and why, though we will also continue to give you suggestions (again, via the Augmented App).

If you can't get enough, or want to have more practice, go to the *Digging Deeper Section* (see page 162).

Larry, forty-one years old and single, lived alone in rural Mississippi in his parents' house, which was now his house, though he couldn't bring himself to think of it that way. He acted more like a curator ... (**17** 6–9)

But even before that, because of his past, Larry hadn't been allowed to own a gun. (**21** 5–6)

And Wallace Stringfellow, of course, who was his only friend. (**22** 21–22)

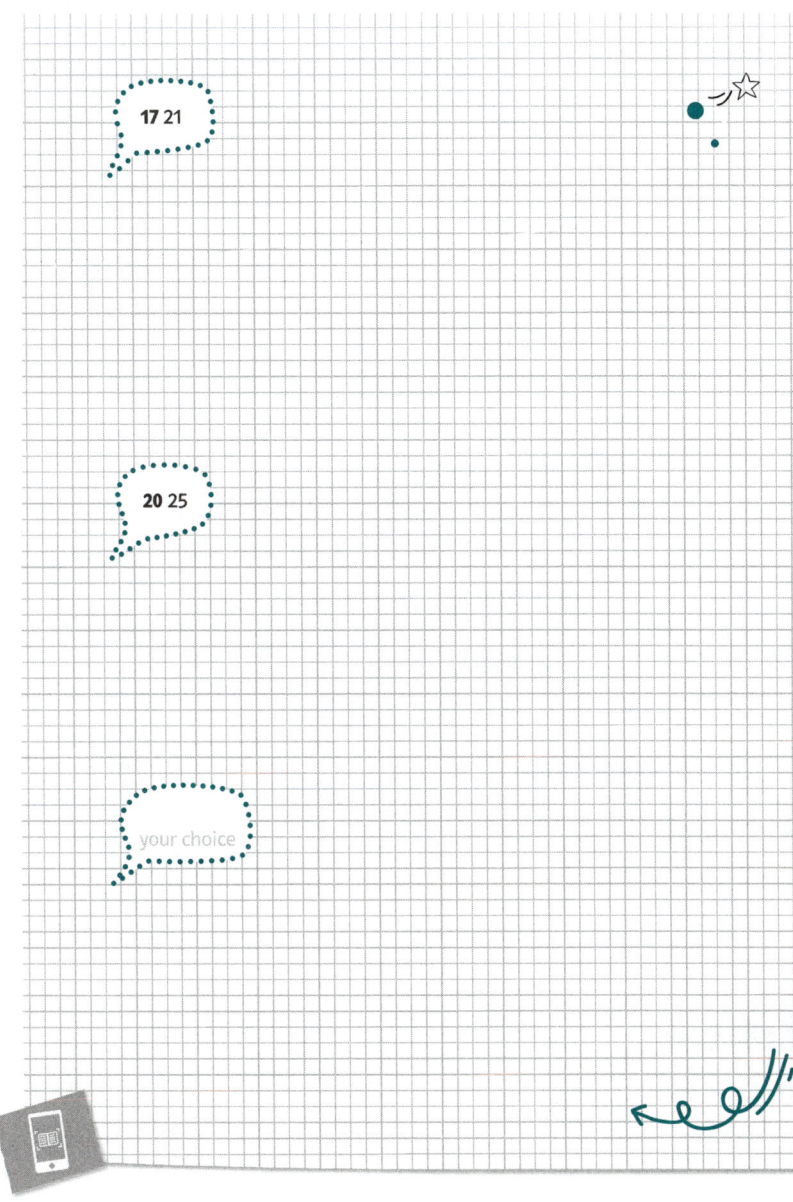

1. Reading Guide

Quote in Context

The following sentences are taken from the most central passage in the novel so far. What happens before? What happens after? Why is this passage so relevant?

Before…

> But he didn't get to deny abducting the Rutherford girl last week, or Cindy Walker twenty-five years ago, because the man stepped closer and jammed the barrel against Larry's chest, Larry for a moment seeing human eyes in the monster's face, something familiar in there. Then he heard the shot.

(23 30 – **24** 3)

After…

Relevance of passage:

Sneak Preview

Hang in there! After the fairly fast beginning of the story, you'll probably find the next chapter rather sluggish and slow-moving. But you'll find out some interesting facts about Larry's past.

Focus is on: ☐ Larry ☐ Silas ☐ both

1.2 Chapter 2 — 30 pages

This chapter is difficult to read. There are many different strands of the story. The description of the swamp is full of atmospheric vocabulary. Set aside at least one hour. The following suggestions will make reading the chapter a bit easier for you (and hopefully more fun, too).

While-reading

Listen to the sounds of the American South while you read pages 28–31 of this chapter (1.2 Swamp sounds).

Also, while you're reading, keep the following questions in mind and maybe even take notes:

Who **likes** whom in Chabot?

Who **dislikes** whom?

What do **you** think it must feel like living in a place like this?

1. Reading Guide

The Story

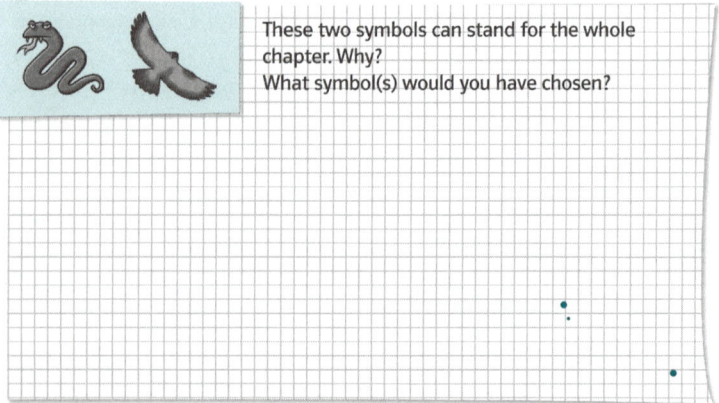

These two symbols can stand for the whole chapter. Why?
What symbol(s) would you have chosen?

Here's a short summary of the second chapter. Due to its rather bloody and unsavory nature, it's difficult to read. Can you make it legible again?

Summary

We meet Silas, a police constable in Chabot, Mississippi. His nickname is '32', his number when he played base███ Silas is rather popular, Afro-american and he likes sp███ He seems to be the com███ opposite of Larry Ott.

He is looking for Tina Rutherford, the missing d███er of the local mill ███r. Alarmed by a flock of birds, Silas decides to investigate and finds a co███e in the process. Lying in the swamp, bloated and half-eaten, is M&M, an old s███ acquaintance and local dr██ dealer. The p███e constable also helps Iri██ an attractive young woman who keeps flirting ███ him, by removing a snake from her ███lbox.

███llowing Silas' instructions, his girlfriend Angie ██s Larry injured and unconscious in his own house.

bloody and unsavory
blutig und unappetitlich

Characters

Jot down the names of the new characters in this chapter. Add some very basic information about them.

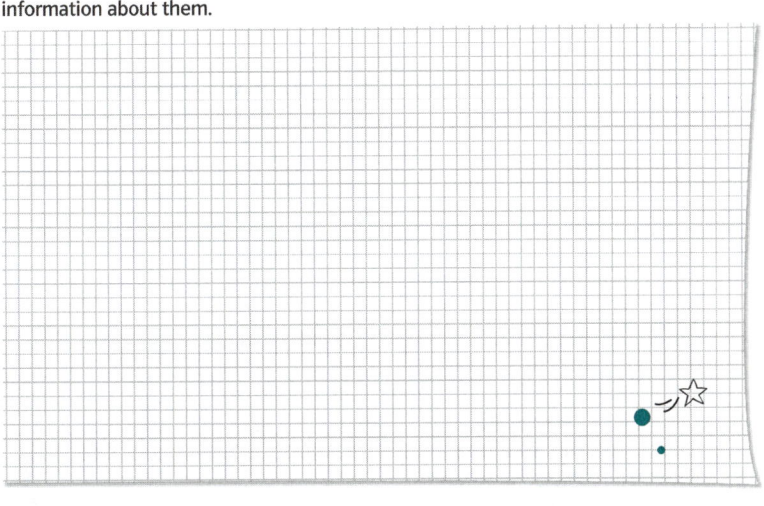

 Go to page 124 in Section 2 and take some notes on Silas Jones.

What are the **main differences** between Larry and Silas? Make a list:

Larry Ott	Silas Jones

Quotes

What points are these quotes making?

> He thought of his mother, dead eight years. The time the two of them lived in a hunting cabin on land owned by a white man. No water in the place, no electricity, no gas. They'd been squatters there ... (**29** 13–15)

> Chabot didn't have an ATM; the nearest was eleven miles north, in Fulsom. Cell phones worked in Chabot sometimes and sometimes they didn't. (**38** 21–23)

> That, in high school, a girl who lived up the road from Larry had gone to the drive-in movie with him and nobody had seen her again. (**45** 31–33)

40 31–41 5

43 17–20

51 3–6

1. Reading Guide

Vocab & Language

➢ Here are **ten important words** from these pages.
What do they mean? Translate or explain.

buzzard	
to insinuate ys into	
plaid	
to flip on sb	
DUI	
premeditated	
to take a hint	
clammy	
to ostracise	
copperhead	

➢ Note down expressions or phrases that you like and might want to recycle in your own writing:

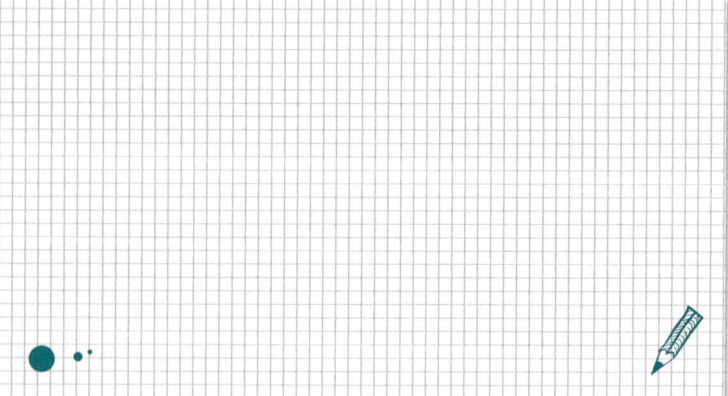

➢ Write down **three words** from this chapter that

are completely irrelevant to you:	you **like the sound of**:	you'd like to remember:
▸	▸	▸
▸	▸	▸
▸	▸	▸

··

Talk about it! Useful words to describe this chapter:

hint   flashback   isolation   decline   atmosphere   cliffhanger

Talk about it! A place can be said to...

have seen better days   be in decline   be depressing
be decaying   be destitute   be bleak

Talk about it! The air can be...

hot   humid   stifling
muggy   sticky   sultry
tropical   sweltering   stuffy

 **Clues**

While you are reading the novel, you sort of turn into a detective yourself and can collect clues. Which clues to the various crimes have you found so far?

 Go to Section 3 (p. 130) and keep track of the clues scattered throughout the novel.

Over to you

One interpretation of "**the ambiguity of belonging**" might be that people want to belong to a certain peer group but for some reason cannot. Look at the first 30 pages again and find examples of who belongs where or to whom. What are reasons that people can't belong?

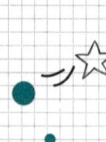

How do you feel about the novel so far? What's it like reading it? What about the atmosphere of the place? How do you feel about the characters? Anyone you like or particularly dislike? How would you like the story to go on?

While reading the first part of the chapter, you listened to some sounds from the American South. What did you think about them? Was this useful while reading or did it get on your nerves? If this helped, why don't you compile a soundtrack to listen to while you read the book? Which songs would you include?

Sneak Preview

Congratulations – you've made it! From now on, all the other chapters will seem like a walk in the park. Talking about a walk in the park, the next chapter features a lot of walks in the woods. Read on to find out more.

1. Reading Guide

1.3 Chapter 3 – 26 pages

The story

  These two symbols can stand for the whole chapter. Why? What symbol(s) would you have chosen?

Here's a word cloud that goes with Chapter 3. Try and retell the plot using the words given here.

Summary

Quotes

What points are these quotes making?

"Larry," the woman said, as if she knew him, "this is Silas. Silas, this is Larry."
(**57** 9)

"You've never minded," Larry's mother said to Alice, looking hard at her, "using other people's things."
(**61** 13–14)

He understood that Carl liked most everyone except him.
(**61** 25)

69 18–23

80 7–9

your choice

Jot down the names of the **new characters** in this chapter.
Add some very basic information about them.

Vocab & Language

➢ Here are **ten important words** from these pages.
What do they mean? Translate or explain.

inappropriate	
freezing	
curious	
to betray / betrayal	
mechanically disinclined	
a convertible	
to glimpse	
to segregate	
a whipping	
reverence	

1. Reading Guide

➢ Note down expressions or phrases that you like and might want to recycle in your own writing:

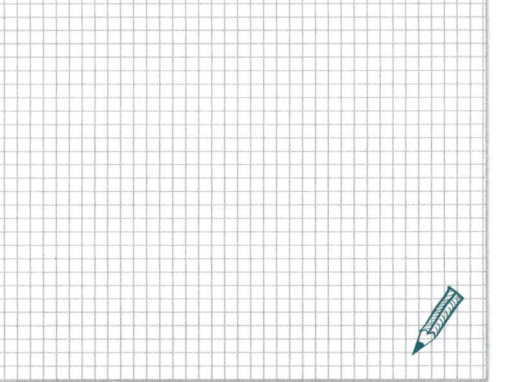

➢ Write down **three words** from this chapter that

are completely irrelevant to you:	you **like the sound of**:	you'd like **to remember**:
▶	▶	▶
▶	▶	▶
▶	▶	▶

Talk about it! Useful words to describe this chapter:

trying to fit it	struggling for acceptance	to befriend sb
clumsy	kindness	masculinity

Sneak Preview

Here's a quote from the next chapter. Read on and follow Silas through Larry's house. "There it was. The barn. He stood leaning on the gate and saw himself years ago, the day he'd come here. No grownups, no teachers, no other girls or boys, black or white, just him and Larry. He remembered following Larry through the house." (**87** 18–23)

Focus is on: ☐ Larry ☐ Silas ☐ both

1.4 Chapter 4 – 15 pages

The story

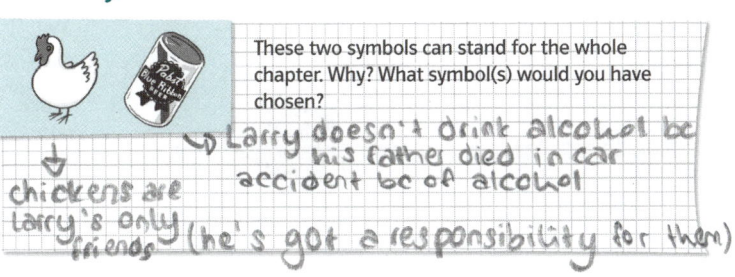

These two symbols can stand for the whole chapter. Why? What symbol(s) would you have chosen?

Larry doesn't drink alcohol bc his father died in car accident bc of alcohol

chickens are Larry's only friends (he's got a responsibility for them)

While reading the chapter, fill in the correct words to complete the short summary.

Summary

After speaking to Angie, ... finds out that .... has been taken to hospital and is in a .... He drives out to Larry's house and .... , investigating the living quarters and the .... Silas is impressed with how .... the place is. He .... that Larry has become isolated and .... with only his .... and .... Remembering his boyhood and their .... , he moves from room to room .... finds nothing unusual. Chief French arrives and they talk about Larry's strangeness. They wonder about the .... in Larry's fridge and about the .... that he was not allowed to own. When Silas .... home, there is a short, important .... from Larry on his ....

answering machine – barn – beer – books – but – chickens – coma– companions – friendship – gets – gun – Larry – looks around – lonely – message – neat – realizes – Silas

Quotes

Find some **key sentences** in Chapter 4. Why do you think they are important?

Clues

The following clues are given in this chapter. What do you as a detective make of them? Take some notes:

The beer in the fridge:

The gun on the floor:

The message on Silas' answering machine:

1. Reading Guide

Vocab & Language

➢ Here are **ten important words** from these pages.
What do they mean? Translate or explain.

a puddle of blood	
hunch	
jurisdiction	
decline	
to board up	
ancient	
neat	
to incarcerate	
tire print	
self-inflicted	

....

➢ Note down expressions or phrases that you like and might want to recycle in your own writing:

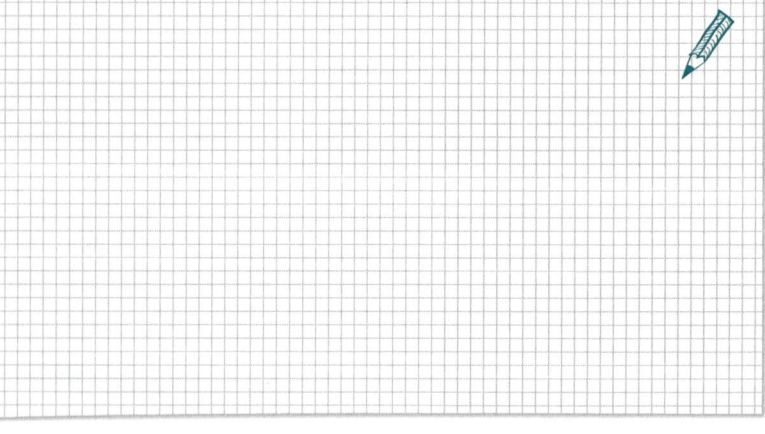

➢ Write down **three words** from this chapter that

are completely irrelevant to you:	you **like the sound of:**	you'd like to remember:
▶	▶	▶
▶	▶	▶
▶	▶	▶

over to you

 How do you feel about Larry? What might have happened?

 What do you think could have happened to Larry and Silas' friendship?

There are various assaults and fights in the next chapter.
It's a real page-turner…

1. Reading Guide

Focus is on: ☐ Larry ☐ Silas ☐ both

1.5   Chapter 5 – 24 pages

The story

These two symbols can stand for the whole chapter. Why? What symbol(s) would you have chosen?

rifle

 Collecting clues

As you read through this chapter, try and think like a detective.
What do you learn about Cecil, Carl, Silas and Larry? Who would be your main suspect? Why do you feel they might have been able to commit a crime?

Take notes in Section 3 *Clues* (p. 130 ff.).

Which of the following statements about Chapter 5 are true (T), which are false (F)? Tick them while you are reading the chapter.

Summary

	T	F
1. On a Saturday, Larry and his mum usually ask Carl whether Larry can accompany him to the garage.	☒	☐
2. On the particular Sunday described in Chapter 5, Larry desperately wants to join his father at the garage.	☐	☒
3. Silas and Larry often meet in the woods and play together.	☒	☐
4. They both share a love of snakes and baseball.	☐	☒
5. Larry's idea of 'race' has been influenced by the notion of white supremacy.	☒	☐
6. Larry is aware of the fact that Silas has other interests and tries hard to stay interesting for his friend.	☒	☐
7. Both Carl and Cecil are described as heavy drinkers.	☒	☐
8. Silas and Larry help Cindy when Cecil bothers her.	☐	☒
9. Carl offers the two boys a fair way of deciding who can keep the gun.	☐	☒
10. When Larry cannot fight with his fists he uses the one weapon he excels at – his words.	☒	☐

Quotes

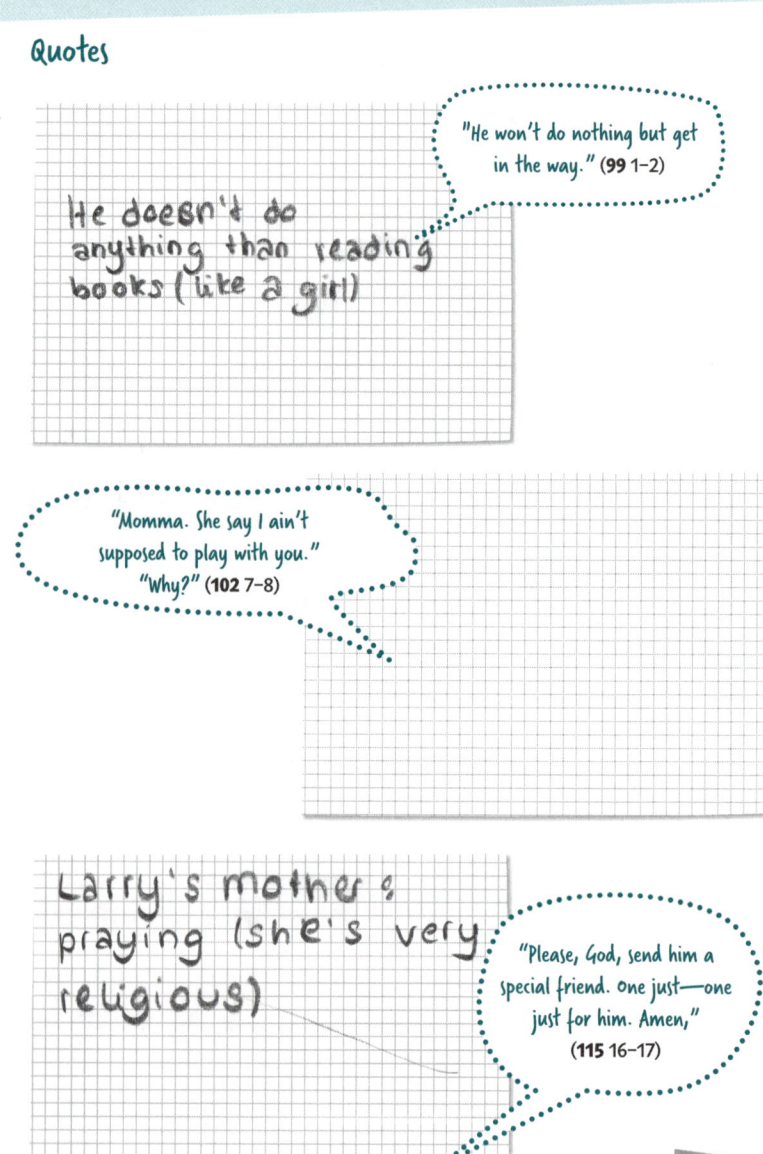

"He won't do nothing but get in the way." (**99** 1–2)

He doesn't do anything than reading books (like a girl)

"Momma. She say I ain't supposed to play with you."
"Why?" (**102** 7–8)

Larry's mother & praying (she's very religious)

"Please, God, send him a special friend. One just—one just for him. Amen," (**115** 16–17)

99 18–20

Carl to Larry
→ relationship is bad/broken
→ he doesn't want him
   to read

120 5–6

your choice

1. Reading Guide

Vocab & Language

➤ Find the **words** in this chapter that match these definitions.
You can do this as you're reading the chapter – they are in chronological order.

definition	word
to work together, to collaborate	
to not succeed, to disappoint the expectations or trust of sb	
to attack by surprise from a hidden place	
a removable covering for a pillow	
to exchange	
the space between a woman's breasts	
to live in a building or on land without the owner's permission and without paying	
acting too quickly, eager, impatient	
suitable for girls but not for boys; having the qualities of a girl	
intensity, violence	

Talk about it! Useful words to describe this chapter:

Useful words to talk about this chapter center around the words
suspect/suspicion. Create a mind map while you read.

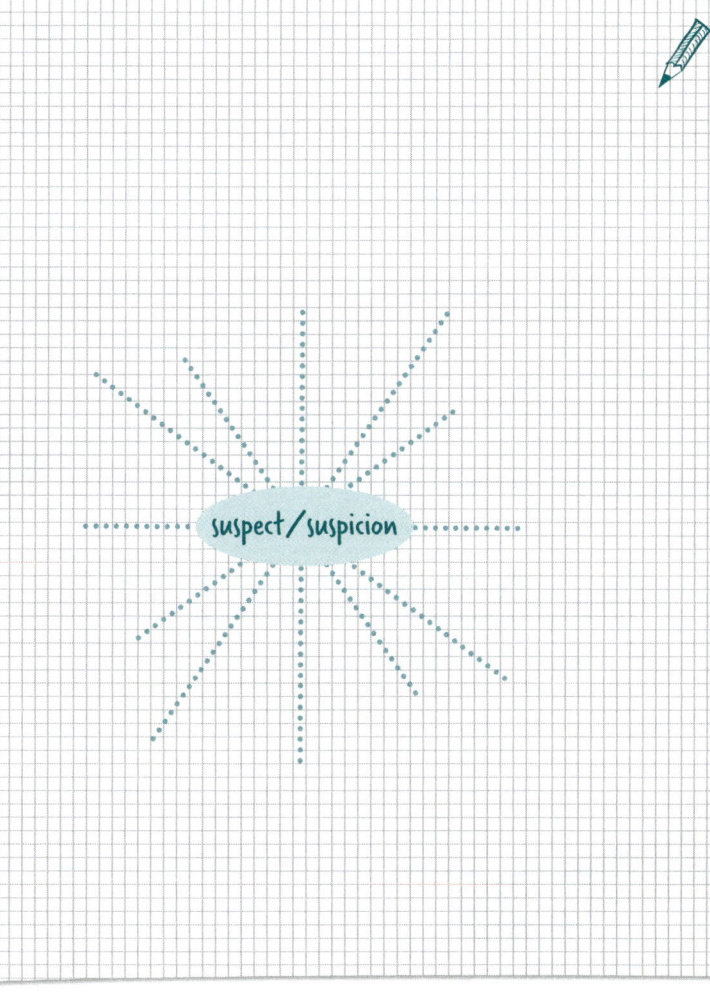

I. Reading Guide

➤ Note down expressions or phrases that you like and might want to recycle in your own writing:

➤ Write down **three words** from this chapter that

are completely irrelevant to you:	you **like the sound of**:	you'd like to remember:
▸	▸	▸
▸	▸	▸
▸	▸	▸

The next chapter talks about how Silas moved down South. Also, Silas makes quite an incredible discovery in Larry's attic ....

Focus is on: ☐ Larry ☐ Silas ☐ both

1.6 Chapter 6 – 24 pages

The story

These two symbols can stand for the whole chapter. Why? What symbol(s) would you have chosen?

....

Characters

What do you imagine Larry and Silas look like? Find pictures and stick them in their character profile on p. 122 & 124 in *Section 2 Characters*. Two examples are given in your Augmented files, though the picture of 'Larry' isn't a perfect match but more of a future version of him.

1. Reading Guide

Here's a jumbled summary of chapter six. As you read, put numbers in the boxes to mark the right order.

 Once you put down 11, listen to a soundtrack from the film 'Driving Miss Daisy' (in your Augmented downloads for this chapter).

Summary

Back inside the house, Silas spends a long time looking at Larry's books and magazines, carefully going through all the piles. ◯

Eventually, he sees the attic trapdoor and climbs up. ◯

He figures out how Larry must have moved the chicken pen, and then feeds the chickens. ◯

First, he finds some small pieces of glass. Then he looks at the tire tracks, some of which have an unusual shape. ◯

Going through the shoebox of old photographs, he is struck by one that shows his mother with Larry on her lap. ◯

He thinks back to his own childhood in Chicago and how his mother's then boyfriend, Oliver, was arrested one day. ◯

In the barn, he discovers Larry's fishing rods and remembers how they used to go fishing together. ◯

Silas finds out that Larry had sold his father's land to the lumber company to make up for his lack of funds. ◯

Silas gets shaken out of his recollections by Angie's phone call. He keeps the photograph of Larry and his mother and leaves Larry's house. ◯

Silas talks to Miss Marla and listens to her views on Larry and the crimes before going to the shop to collect more evidence. *①*

Trying to reconstruct Larry's life, he realizes how lonely his former friend has become. ◯

We read about their arduous journey down south and how Silas tried to run away from his mother, causing her grief and losing them most of their possessions. ◯

When he picks up the roach end of a joint, he is sure that someone else must have been there. ◯

Quotes

While you read the chapter, find quotes which match the given explanations.
Give page and line numbers.

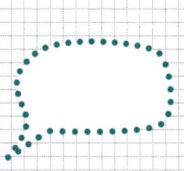

This key sentence gives you a summary of the three crimes so far and how the people in Fulsom / Chabot feel about them.

These lines tell you how people in the village used to treat Larry.

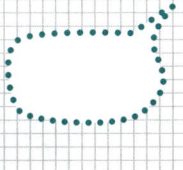

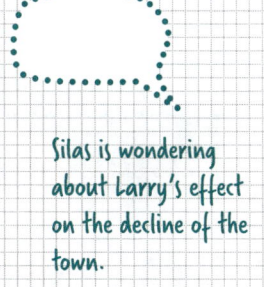

Silas is wondering about Larry's effect on the decline of the town.

This short passage tells Silas that his mother must have worked for Larry's family once.

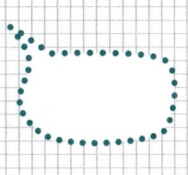

Vocab & Language

➢ Look at the pictures. They all stand for one word from the chapter.
   Label the pictures and think of their relevance in the chapter.

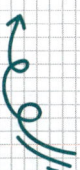

Note down expressions or phrases from this chapter that you like and might want to recycle in your own writing:

___

Talk about it! Useful words to describe this chapter:

memories	recollections	to think of
to think back	to remember	to recollect
to recall	to reminisce about	to be lost in thought

Post-reading

How did the *Driving Miss Daisy* track make you feel?
Which scene in the Chapter does it match best?

What songs do you feel would go well with this chapter? Compile a soundtrack!

Sneak Preview

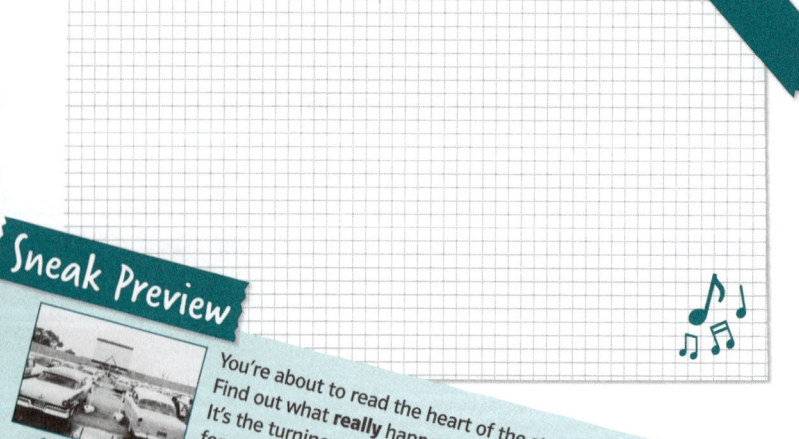

You're about to read the heart of the story now.
Find out what **really** happened at the ominous date.
It's the turning-point in Larry's life. His struggle
for acceptance and belonging to a group
turns sour. Are you ready?

Focus is on: ☐ Larry ☐ Silas ☐ both

1.7 Chapter 7 – 29 pages

Pre-reading

Imagine you're Larry and are going out on a date. What kind of things do you have to plan in advance? What do you need to take along?

Remember: this is before the internet and WhatsApp, so you have very little chance of being spontaneous and need to plan well in advance.

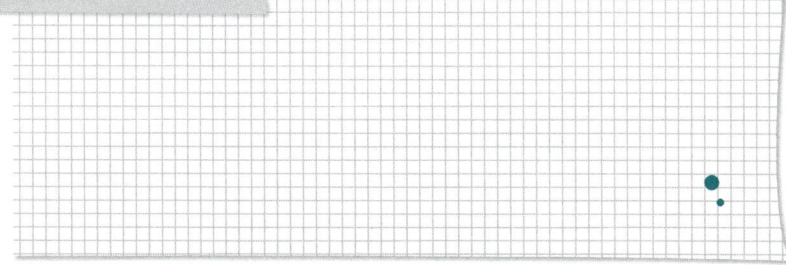

While-reading

As you read, pay attention to how the author tries our patience: Where does he tell 'stories' that slow down the narration to make us wait for the next piece of information? What effect does this have on you as a reader?

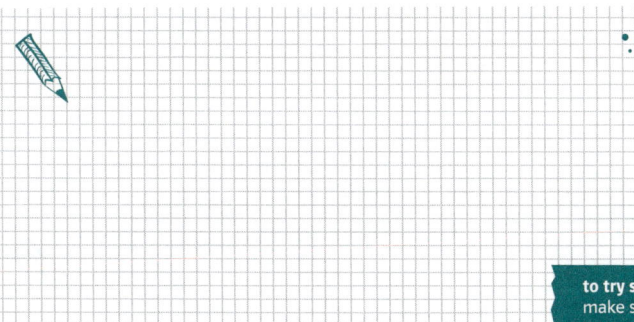

to try sb's patience to make sb angry or annoyed (here: by slowing down the story)

1. Reading Guide

The story

These two symbols can stand for the whole chapter. Why? What symbol(s) would you have chosen?

Listen to *Stayin' Alive* from the BeeGees. (It should be among the files you downloaded for this chapter via the Augmented App.) The song is mentioned in the text. What is the context? Why do you think the author chose this song?

Here's a short summary of the seventh chapter. Fill in the missing words.
They are given in the box below.

Summary

To everybody's surprise and ...., Cindy asks Larry

out .... a date. They want .... go to a drive-in ....

Larry's classmates are totally .... and Larry finally

feels .... The date, however, turns .... to be a

mere .... for Cindy's plan to .... her real

boyfriend. She .... Larry that she is ....

After he drops her .... she is never seen ....

Since he was the .... to see her last, ... finds

himself accused of .... and murdering her.

Following .... allegations against Larry, he .... out

of high school, ... the army where he .... as a

mechanic. His .... business gradually declines

and ...., Carl eventually succumbs to ....

and dies in a .... accident. His mother Ina ....

and eventually suffers from .... When his father

dies, ... returns to Chabot to .... after

Ina but soon .... to move her into a .... home.

abducting – accepted – again – alcohol – amazement – car –
cover-up – dementia – drops – fails – father's – has – impressed
– joins – Larry – Larry – look – meet – movie – nursing – off –
on – one – out – pregnant – tells – the – to – trains – withdraws

1. Reading Guide

Picture-input

Look at the picture of the boy swinging on the rope. Try and retell the story in your own words. What function(s) does this short narrative have?

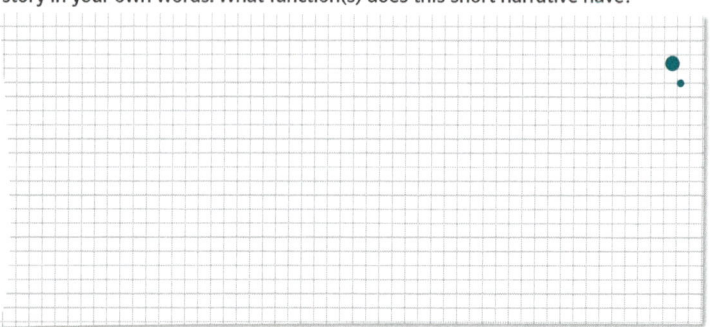

Quotes

Why do you think these quotes might be relevant?

"Larry," his mother said.
"Did you tell Daddy?"
(**145** 18)

"You a badass now?"
(**152** 22)

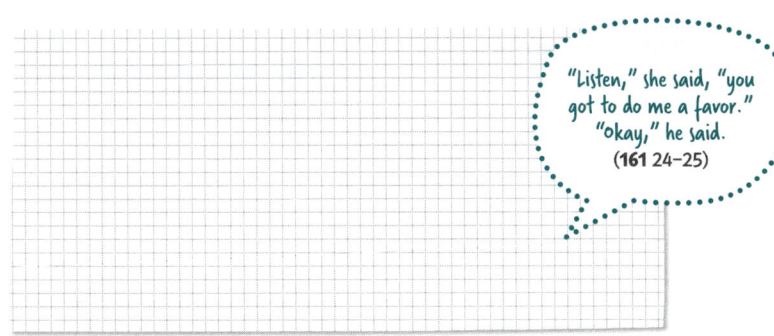

"Listen," she said, "you got to do me a favor."
"okay," he said.
(**161** 24–25)

Find two more meaningful quotes. Outline why you think they are important or worth remembering!

Vocab & Language

➤ Here are some **important words** from these pages. What do they mean?
Translate or explain. They all start with either the letter **C** or the letter **D**.
Why do you think these words were chosen to represent this chapter?
Add more C and D words to the list.

C is for	D is for
Cindy	date
Cecil	difference
catastrophe	disappearance
chaos	drive-in
cover-up	disaster
cinema	

➤ Note down expressions or phrases from this chapter that you like and might
want to recycle in your own writing:

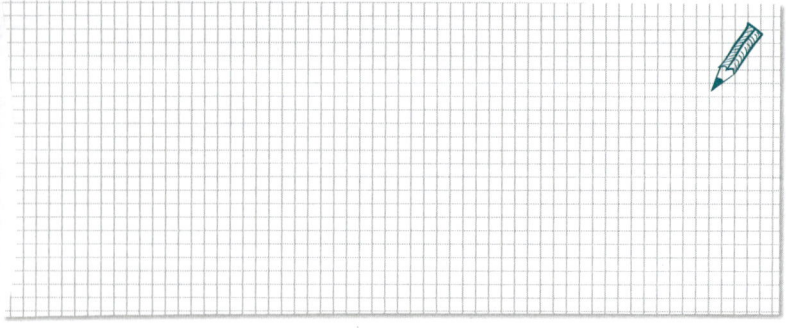

➤ Write down **three words** from this chapter that

are completely irrelevant to you:	you **like the sound of**:	you'd like to remember:
▸	▸	▸
▸	▸	▸
▸	▸	▸

Talk about it! Useful words to describe Larry's emotions

"First I was afraid, I was petrified …."

happy	proud	pleased	surprised	amazed
nervous	excited	over the moon	shocked	speechless
tricked	disappointed	all revved up and no place to go		

Over to you

How do you feel about Cindy's plan?

Why do you think Larry played along? Could he have reacted differently?

1. Reading Guide

This is the cliffhanger at the end of the chapter:

> **❝** ... seldom thinking of his mother's old prayer, the one where she asked God to send him a special friend. Until it was answered. **❞**
>
> (**173** 28–30)

How do you imagine the story to go on?

Sneak Preview

The next chapter (Chapter 8) ends with these lines:

"Somebody had been inside, he saw now. There was a long smear over the floor. His pulse quickened as he imagined the intruder dragging his feet to erase his tracks. He fixed his beam beneath the bed. There it was, a shadow image of the bed cast in rumpled dirt, a place where someone had dug, he realized, a grave." (**194** 21–26)

Find out what happens.

1.8 Chapter 8 – 21 pages

The story

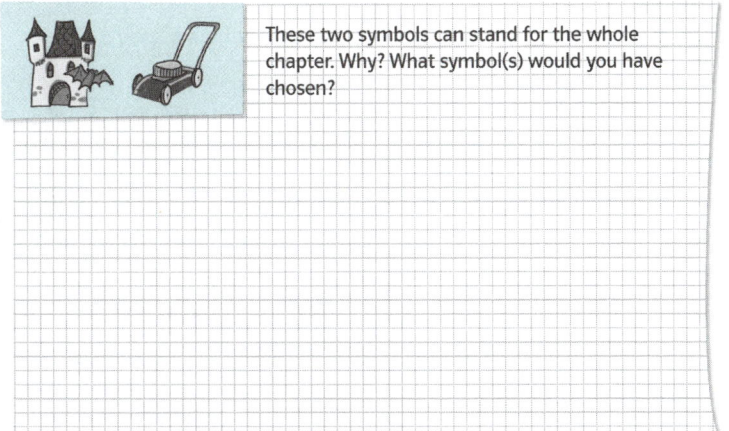

These two symbols can stand for the whole chapter. Why? What symbol(s) would you have chosen?

Here's another wordle to go with the chapter. Use it to re-tell the plot in your own words.

Summary

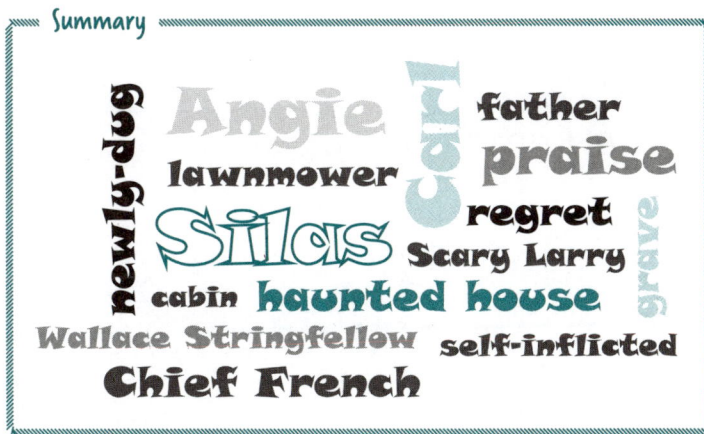

Quotes

Look at the quote below. How does this fit into the notion of *the ambiguity of belonging*?

> I felt like I belonged here. It's part of why I came back, after all that time. I'd never forgot this place.
>
> **(176** 6–7)

Find three more passages or quotes in this chapter that you find meaningful or important. Outline why.

your choice

your choice

your choice

Vocab & Language

Find the following words and expressions while reading the chapter.
What do they mean? Come up with a translation or synonym.

word / expression	translation / synonym
to nab	
to snap	
a hick	
to knock up	
by the breadth of a hair	
to dote over sb	
weathered	
beam	
intruder	
rumpled	

➢ Note down expressions or phrases that you like and might want to recycle in your own writing:

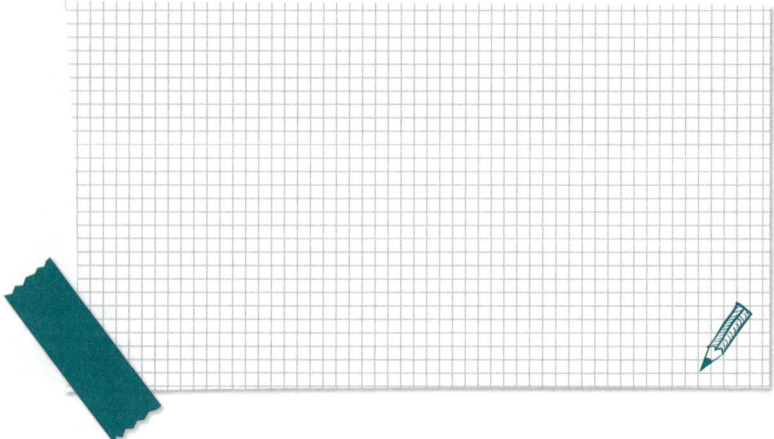

➢ Write down **three words** from this chapter that

are completely irrelevant to you:	you **like the sound of**:	you'd like to remember:
▸	▸	▸
▸	▸	▸
▸	▸	▸

Characters

How do you feel about Wallace Stringfellow. What is your gut feeling? Do you feel the narrator manipulates your feelings about Wallace? Why / Why not?

Sneak Preview Are you ready to find out more about Wallace Stringfellow? Then read Chapter 9 …

1. Reading Guide

1.9   Chapter 9 – 29 pages

 Pre-reading

a)   Who is your best friend?

b)   Where and how did you meet?

c)   Why do you think you became friends?

d)   Define: A friend is someone who ….

The story

These two symbols can stand for the whole chapter. Why? What symbol(s) would you have chosen?

Put these sentences in the right order for a coherent summary of this chapter.

Summary

Wallace gives Larry a gun for Christmas ⭘

This boy was Wallace Stringfellow, who now returns, ⭘

pretending to work for a TV company, to strike up a friendship with Larry. ⭘

Larry recalls how he once used his monster mask to scare a young boy from his barn. ①

Larry is hungry for human contact and enjoys Wallace's visits ⭘

in spite of the younger man smoking drugs and drinking too much. ⭘

and visits him on New Year's Eve, too. ⭘

– asks Larry weird questions about Cindy Walker's disappearance ⭘

and becomes sexually aroused by the conversation about abducting and raping girls. ⭘

Eventually, Wallace – whose dog is named after a serial killer ⭘

He assaults Larry's car when Larry does not share his enthusiasm. ⭘

1. Reading Guide

 ## Characters

 What do you think Wallace looks like? Find a picture and stick it in here. Add relevant information to Wallace Stringfellow's character profile on pp. 126–127 in Section 2.

 **Quotes**

Read the following quote. What do you think Larry means?
What is implied about 'belonging'?

> Until you ate you didn't know how hungry you were, how empty
> you'd become. Wallace's visits had shown him that being lonesome
> was its own fast, that after going unnourished for so long, even
> the foulest bite could remind your body how much it needed to
> eat. That you could be starving and not even know it.
>
> **(223** 10–15)

Vocab & Language

➢ Here are **ten important words** from these pages. What do they mean? Translate or explain.

aftermath	
to dangle	
to eject	
infamous	
lump	
ratty	
scruffy	
thigh	
toddler	
wondrous	

➢ Note down expressions or phrases that you like and might want to recycle in your own writing:

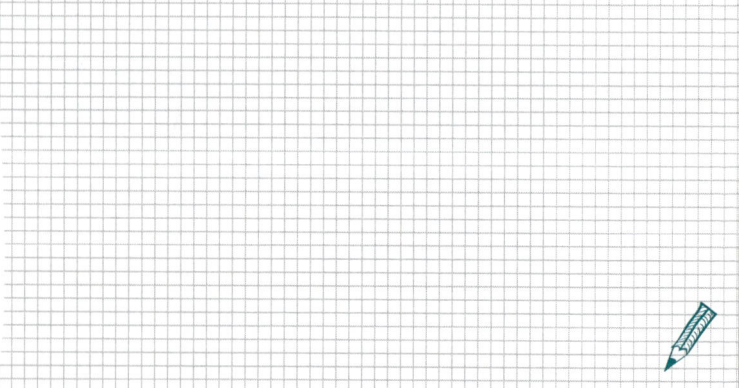

➢ Write down **three words** from this chapter that

are completely irrelevant to you:	you **like the sound of**:	you'd like **to remember**:
▸	▸	▸
▸	▸	▸
▸	▸	▸

Talk about it! Useful words to describe this chapter:

Come up with a mind map based on the word "friendship"?

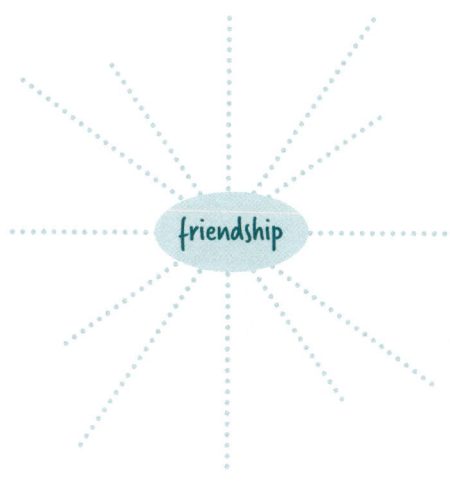

friendship

Post-reading

Wallace Stringfellow

After reading this chapter, how do you feel about Wallace Stringfellow? Complete the sentences.

I have the feeling that ....

My hunch is that ....

I expect Wallace to ....

Sneak Preview

If the novel was turned into a film, you'd next find yourself watching three important scenes: First, a conversation between Angie and Silas in a pizza place, then Larry in a coma, and finally Mrs. Ott in the nursing home.

1.10   Chapter 10 – 28 pages

The story

These two symbols can stand for the whole chapter. Why? What symbol(s) would you have chosen?

↳pizza: Silas eats it with Angie (his gf)
↳ bed: under it the dead body is found;
          Larry lying in coma (in a bed)

After you have read the chapter, listen to the summary provided with the Augmented downloads. It contains four mistakes. Find them and correct them on the lines provided.

Summary

Silas has found .... in ....

In hospital he tells Larry ....

Angie ....

I. Reading Guide

Quotes

Here's a passage from the novel that sums up the state of the investigation so far. What's your own view? You might also want to add notes to *Section 3 Clues* on p. 130 ff.

> But despite the fact that no more bones had been found, reporters and newscasters were speculating that Larry Ott had attempted suicide because of what he'd done to Tina Rutherford and possibly Cindy Walker and, who knew, maybe other girls.
>
> (**229** 14–18)

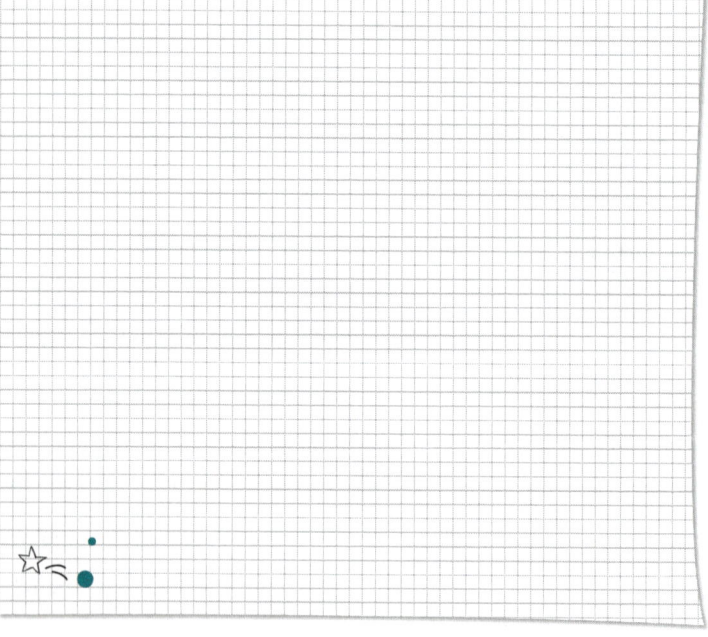

Here are two more **key sentences** from this chapter. Why might they be
important when talking about Silas' and Larry's relationship?

... if he ever woke up.
Sometimes he couldn't
help but wish he wouldn't.
(231 19–20)

I don't know if you can hear me,
Larry, but when you wake up it's gone
be bad. ... Don't tell them nothing,
Larry, you hear? Hear? They gone try
to get you to confess, but don't say
nothing, Larry. Hear? Nothing.
(231 25–30)

1. Reading Guide

Over to you

 How do you think Silas feels after his conversation with Angie?
What do you make of her reaction?

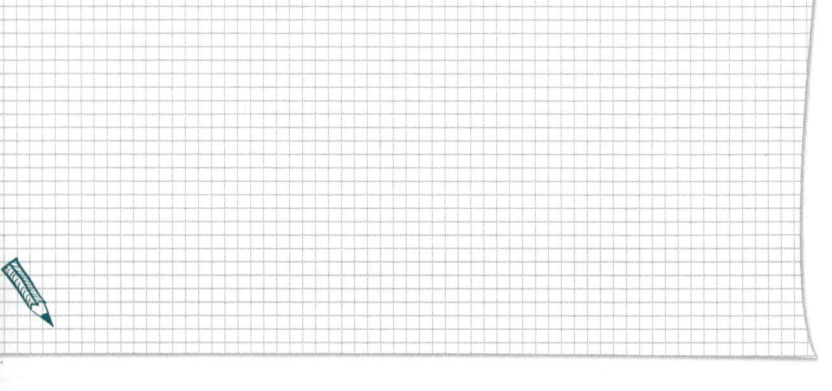

Vocab & Language

➤ Here are **ten important words** from these pages. Translate or explain.
What do they have in common?

crave	
grief	
impatient	
ire	
pant	
peeved	
rant	
retch	
starve	
worried	

➢ Note down expressions or phrases that you like and might want to recycle in your own writing:

➢ Write down **three words** from this chapter that

are completely irrelevant to you:	you **like the sound of**:	you'd like **to remember**:
▸	▸	▸
▸	▸	▸
▸	▸	▸

 Sneak Preview

After Silas has told him not to confess, Larry wakes up from his coma … and the police are there. What will he tell them?

1. Reading Guide

1.11   Chapter 11 – 10 pages

The story

These two symbols can stand for the whole chapter. Why? What symbol(s) would you have chosen?

This summary of Chapter 11 is made up of different short quotes only. As you read through the chapter, find the right order. Then use the list to re-tell the plot.

You could record your summary and send it to a friend.

Summary

"Can I talk . . ." He swallowed. "To Silas?"   ○

"Did they find that girl?"   ○

"Did you shoot yourself?"   ○

"Do you think I did it?"   ○

"He saved your life, Larry."   ○

"It's amazing you're still with us   ○

"Maybe that's why you shot yourself, Larry. All that guilt, adding up   ○

"Okay. We all remember things different, I guess."   ○

"Stay with us, Larry, stay with us."   ①

"We were friends," Larry said.   ○

"Yeah. I do, Larry. I think you done away with both girls. Tina Rutherford and Cindy Walker: ○

smoked a little dope, got out of your head, and next thing you know you've taken her. Just to talk, for all I know. Little companionship. Man gets lonely   ○

You had, if memory serves, bout three and a half hours when you was unaccounted for,...   ○

1. Reading Guide

Quotes

Here are four more **key sentences** from Chapter 11. Why might they be relevant?

> He'd been dreaming about him and Silas, perched in high branches. Then it was him and Wallace. **(252** 1–2)

> But we ain't never found nothing to let us convict you for that Walker girl or any other girls. Till now. **(259** 18–20)

> Hell, maybe we all partly to blame, whole county ostracizing you. Maybe you just wanted some company. **(259** 31–33)

> I don't know anybody except my momma and she don't know me. **(261** 26–27)

Vocab & Language

➢ Seeing as we're in Chapter 11, here are **eleven important words** that all have to do with feeling ill, weak, drifting in and out of consciousness. What do they mean? Translate or explain.

chapped	
distorted	
dizziness	
hoarse	
to blur	
to convulse	
to fade	
to float	
to gag	
to rasp	
to sip	

➢ Note down expressions or phrases that you like and might want to recycle in your own writing:

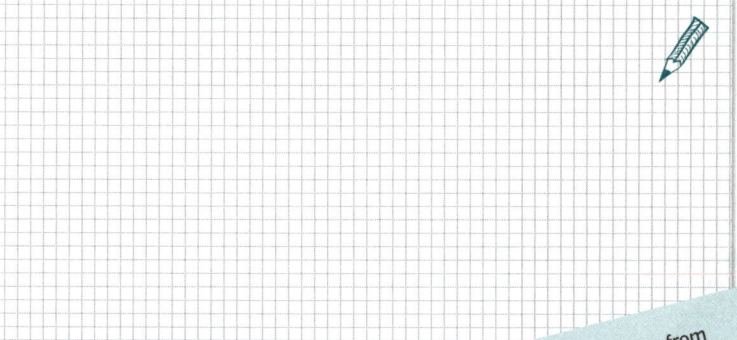

Sneak Preview

Remember the mailbox incident with the snake from the beginning of the novel? Well, you can find out more about it in Chapter 12.

1. Reading Guide

Focus is on: ☐ Larry ☒ Silas ☐ both

1.12 Chapter 12 – 14 pages

The story

These two symbols can stand for the whole chapter. Why? What symbol(s) would you have chosen?

tight friendship of Silas & Larry
→ both apologize → find back to each other

Friendship

!ABI

In this chapter Silas and Larry meet again after not having seen each other for decades. How do they treat each other? How is the encounter described by the author? How did you feel while reading this?

What aspects of 'friendship' are reflected?

In this chapter Silas has a lot of encounters with others. Add arrows and label them with the relevant verbal expressions provided. You can also add information on other characters that you find relevant!

confesses being with Cindy – takes off case – apologizes for sth he said – doesn't think of X as a 'friend' – stays loyal to – reveals sth about Wallace – tries to seduce

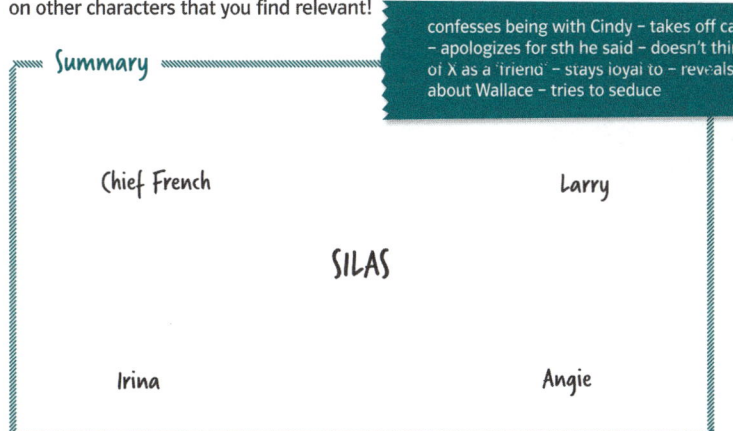

~~~ Summary ~~~

Chief French   Larry

SILAS

Irina   Angie

Quotes

Outline what is meant by these two quotes:

"Horror, it ain't my thing. Too much of that in real life." (**265** 1)

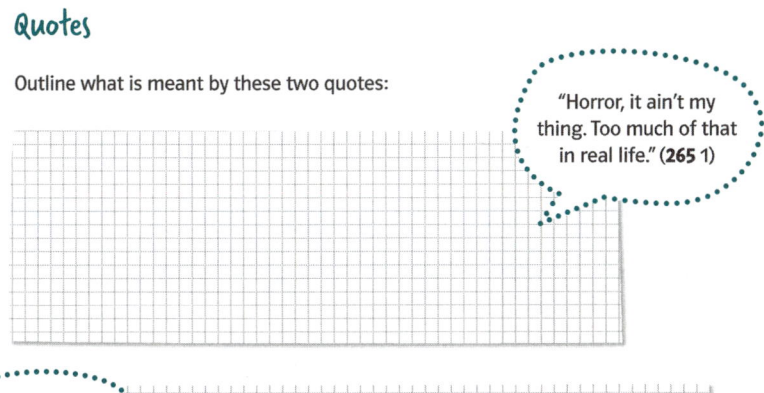

"Larry's done time his whole life". (**269** 20)

Find three more passages that you think are meaningful. Jot down why you think so.

Vocab & Language

➤ Here are **some interesting collocations and idioms** from these pages.
What do they mean? Translate or explain.

to craft a confession	craft: make sth. in a skillfull way confession: statement bout having committed a crime
a splotch of color	
to snap sth shut	
to raise your head	
to will sb to do sth	
to witness an interview	
to own up to what you've done	to own up = to admit
to fix sb with a hard gaze	
mounting tension	mounting = growing/rising
to pull your hand away in disgust	disgust: strong feeling of dislike

➤ Note down expressions or phrases from Ch. 12 that you like and might want
to recycle in your own writing:

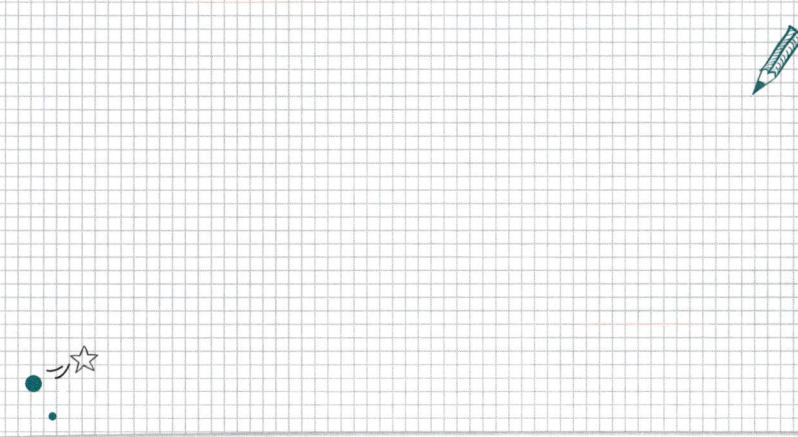

1. Reading Guide

➢ Write down **three words** from chapter 12 that

are completely irrelevant to you:	you **like the sound of**:	you'd like **to remember**:
▸	▸	▸
▸	▸	▸
▸	▸	▸

 over to you

Imagine you are Larry. How would you feel about Silas' confession?

Sneak Preview

In the next chapter, the author brings the puzzle pieces and clues together. Larry is beginning to change. Parts of the chapter are almost like a music video, with a large number of different pictures and sounds. Enjoy!

1.13 Chapter 13 – 8 pages

While-reading

Make sure you always know whether the story is in the present or a flashback to the past.

If you think of this chapter as a 'music video' – which pictures are most vivid in your mind? Outline them here.

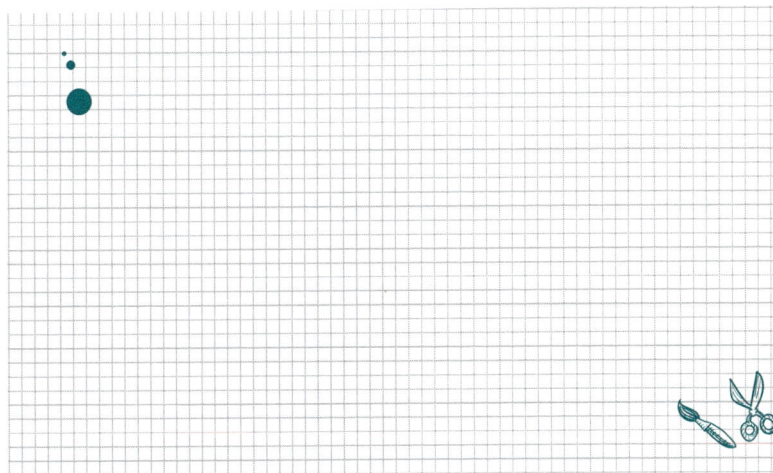

The story

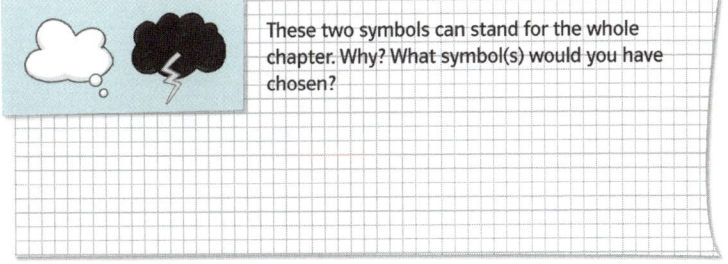

These two symbols can stand for the whole chapter. Why? What symbol(s) would you have chosen?

I. Reading Guide

Write your own short summary of the chapter. Try and use exactly 50 words – this genre is referred to as a 'mini-saga'.

Summary

Clues

What is revealed about the missing girls?
Take notes in the *Clues* section on p. 130 ff.

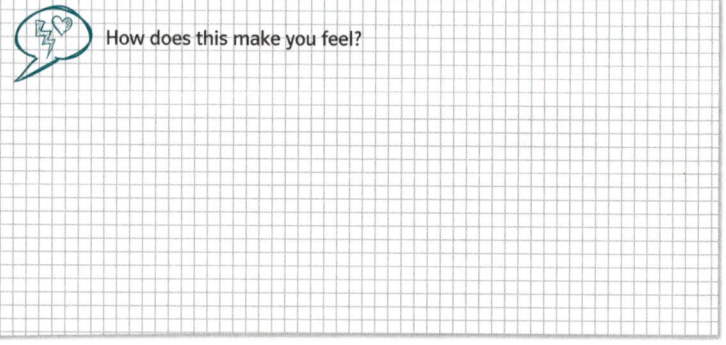

How does this make you feel?

Quotes

What do these key sentences from chapter 13 reveal about 'acceptance'?
Why might they be important?

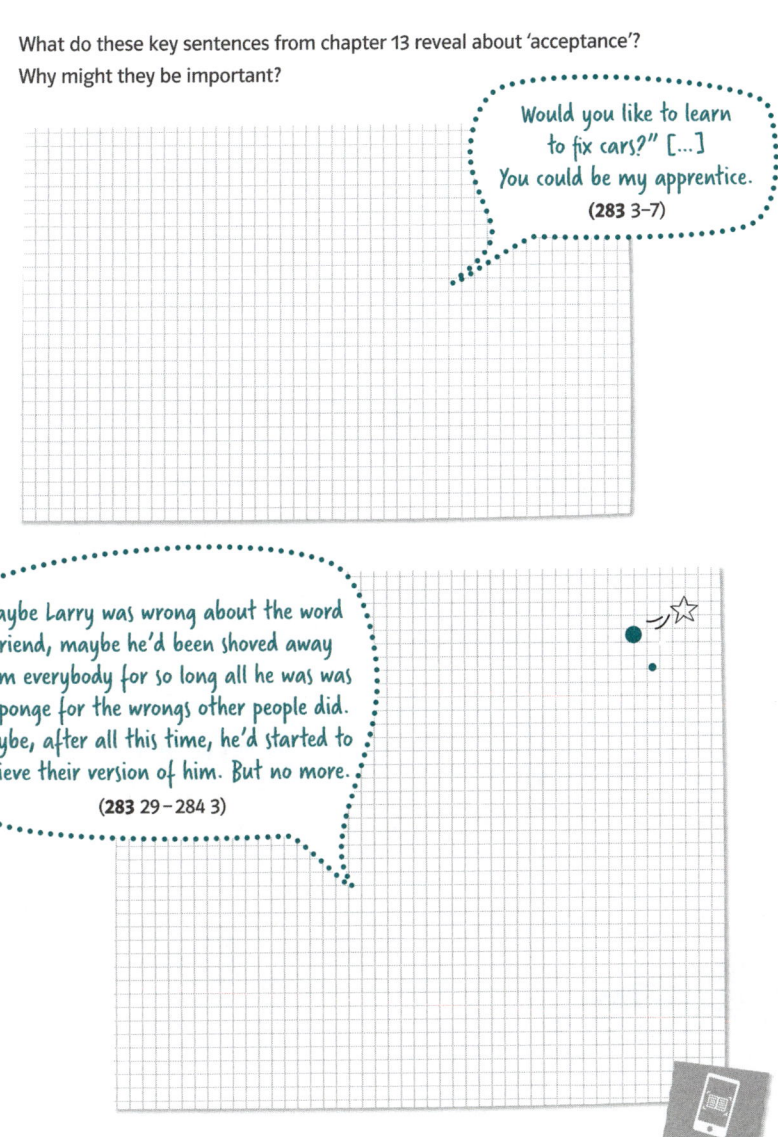

Would you like to learn
to fix cars?" [...]
You could be my apprentice.
(**283** 3–7)

Maybe Larry was wrong about the word
friend, maybe he'd been shoved away
from everybody for so long all he was was
a sponge for the wrongs other people did.
Maybe, after all this time, he'd started to
believe their version of him. But no more.
(**283** 29 – 284 3)

1. Reading Guide

Vocab & Language

➢ Write down five words from these pages you'd like to retain.
What do they mean? Translate or explain.

~~~~ Talk about it! Useful words to describe this chapter: ~~~~

the denouement
to finally understand
everything falls into place
the alleged involvement

to take your fate into your own
  hands
to turn things around
a fresh start – a clean slate

Symbolism

Would you agree that the weather outside is a mirror image of Larry's inner turmoil? Why? Why not?

The sneak preview of the next chapter is an audio file. Listen to 1.13 Sneak preview, then read the next chapter. You're in for an exciting showdown…

1.14 Chapter 14 – 10 pages

The story

These two symbols can stand for the whole chapter. Why? What symbol(s) would you have chosen?

This chapter can be brilliantly summarized by different sounds. Listen to the sound file 1.14 Summary – sounds via your Augmented App and try to retell the scene. You can take notes in the space below.

Summary

1. Reading Guide

Quotes

Guilt

Silas talks about guilt in this chapter. What does he feel guilty about? Why did he get so drunk? What do you think the following passage means?

> The bell over the door rang and she rose with her cigarette. "Well, sugar," she said, limping off, "don't be too hard on yourself. Now and again it's okay to let yourself off the hook." But that was his trouble, wasn't it? Letting himself off the hook had been his way of life.
>
> (**287** 17–21)

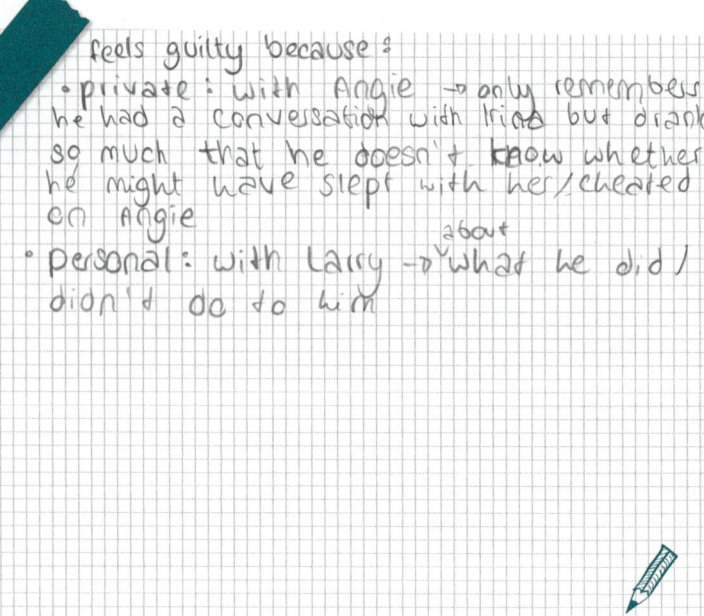

feels guilty because:
- private: with Angie → only remembers he had a conversation with Irina but drank so much that he doesn't know whether he might have slept with her / cheated on Angie
- personal: with Larry → about what he did / didn't do to him

Read p. 290 lines 4–21 and outline how the novel uses foreshadowing as a technique. Write down a few more examples that you have come across while reading the book so far.

> **Foreshadowing** is a literary device in which a writer gives an advance hint of what is to come later in the story. It helps the reader develop expectations about the upcoming events, thus adding dramatic tension.

290 4–21

Vocab & Language

➢ Here are **ten important verbs** from these pages. They're all to do with nerves and guilt and with fighting. What do they mean?
Translate or explain.

to fidget	
to tremble	
to sweat	
to flee	
to back up	
to wrestle	
to clutch	
to bat	
to fumble	
to scrabble	

Find more **verbs of movement** in this chapter. They all contribute to making the story come alive. Things sure move fast here.

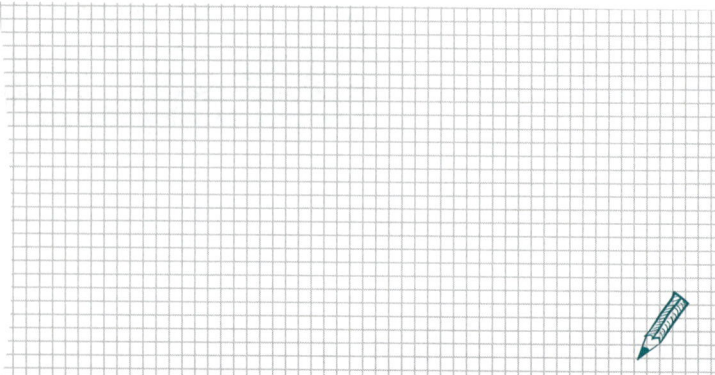

Talk about it! Useful words and phrases to describe this chapter

climax	rising action	to put the pieces together
things fall into place	it finally clicks	Silas confronts Wallace

➢ Write down five words from these pages you'd like to retain.
  What do they mean? Translate or explain.

To find out what happened to Silas and to Wallace **after** the showdown, read on.

1.15 Chapter 15 – 5 pages

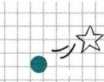

Pre-reading

Imagine you were a counsellor who tries to get Silas and Larry to finally confront their past and talk about the nature of their friendship. Write down **three pieces of advice** you'd give them:

> you need to … – this might be true, but … – I can totally understand why …., however – have you ever thought about …

The story

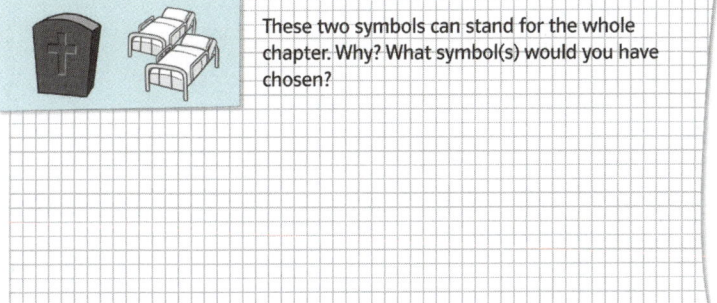

These two symbols can stand for the whole chapter. Why? What symbol(s) would you have chosen?

1. Reading Guide

Create your own wordle for this chapter. Write down the ten most frequent words from the text. Then use the internet, print out your wordle and stick it here on top of your word list.

Summary

Quotes

Here are some **key sentences** from this short chapter. Why are they important?

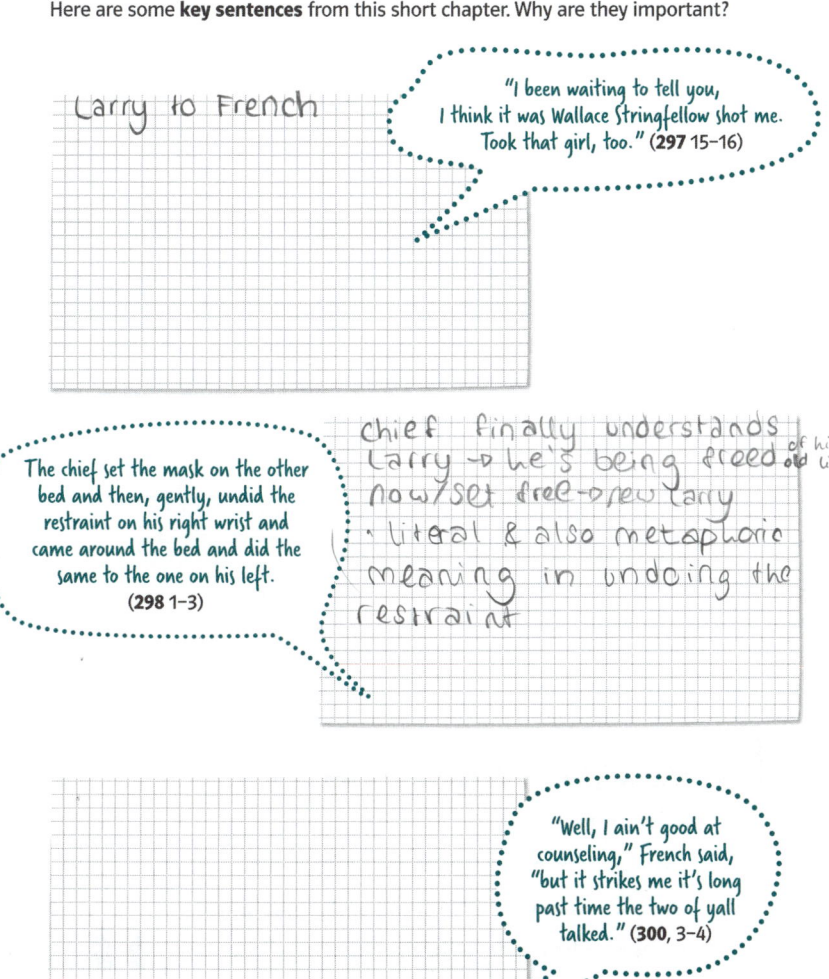

Larry to French

> "I been waiting to tell you,
> I think it was Wallace Stringfellow shot me.
> Took that girl, too." (**297** 15–16)

> The chief set the mask on the other bed and then, gently, undid the restraint on his right wrist and came around the bed and did the same to the one on his left.
> (**298** 1–3)

chief finally understands
Larry → he's being freed of his old life
now/set free → new Larry
· literal & also metaphoric
  meaning in undoing the
restraint

> "Well, I ain't good at counseling," French said, "but it strikes me it's long past time the two of yall talked." (**300**, 3–4)

I. Reading Guide

Find two passages that talk about **friendship.** What is their essence?

! ABI

What does the following passage tell you about the notion of belonging?

"We were both lonesome," he said. "I think that's why he came to see me in the first place. I don't think he had anybody to look up to, a daddy or uncle, and crazy as it sounds, he chose me."

(**299** 20–23)

! ABI

Vocab & Language

➢ Here are **ten important words** from these pages. What do they mean?
Translate or explain.

bridge of the nose	
emulate	
incinerator	
investigate	
lonesome	
option	
rabies	
sap	
speak in low tones	
untangle	

➢ Note down expressions or phrases that you like and might want to recycle in
your own writing:

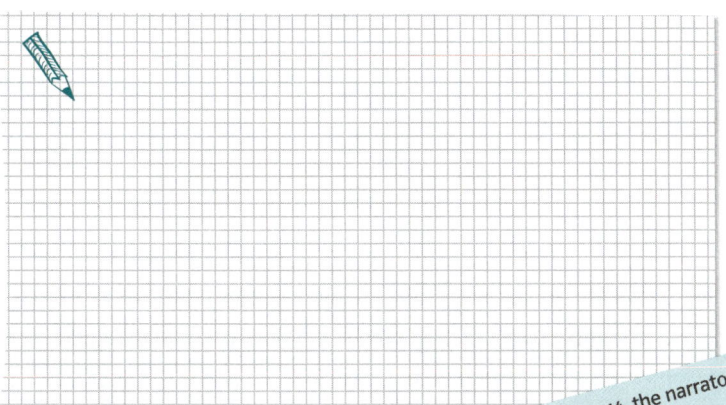

Sneak Preview After the cliffhanger at the end of Chapter 14, the narrator
creates suspense in Chapter 15 by not giving us the
information we want. Does he do this in Chapter 16, too?
Just another hour or so and you'll have finished the book –
congratulations!

1.16   Chapter 16 – 5 pages

💬 Pre-reading

Speculate: how do you think Larry is going to react when he realizes that Silas wants to make up for all the years of friendship that they missed? Will he accept the peace offering, or will he decline and withdraw into his loneliness?

The story

These two symbols can stand for the whole chapter. Why? What symbol(s) would you have chosen?

Here's a summary of the chapter. Use a pen to separate the words:

Summary

LarryandSilasareinhospitaltogetherLarryisfinallyclearedof
thecrimesandbothFrenchandAngieapologizeforwhathehad
toendureLarryandSilasbothrealizetheyarehalfbrothers.

Quotes

> Silas had followed her, still not seeing what an emblem of defeat, shame, loss, hopelessness, the coat was.
>
> **(305** 4–6)

Explain in your own words:
The coat is an emblem of …

emblem symbol

defeat because …

shame because …

loss because …

hopelessness because …

1. Reading Guide

Vocab & Language

➤ Here are **ten important words** from these pages. What do they mean? Translate or explain.

a surprising turn	
allegedly	
apprehend	
attached	
buzzer	
defeat	
flickering TV	
to mute	
occupant	
pursue	

➤ Note down expressions or phrases that you like and might want to recycle in your own writing:

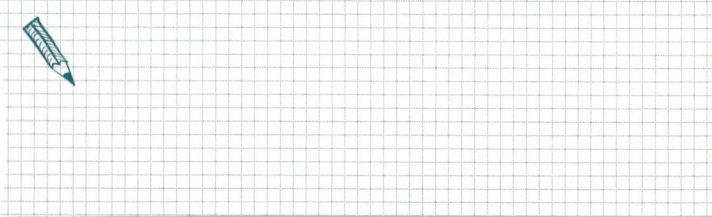

Talk about it! Useful words to talk about this chapter:

to accept an apology   atonement
to seek absolution   to plead with someone

Sneak Preview

How can people possibly apologize or regain some sense of normalcy? Find out whether Larry will continue to sulk.

to sulk to be angry or upset about sth and unwilling to discuss it with other people *(schmollen)*

Focus is on: ☐ Larry ☐ Silas ☐ both

1.17 Chapter 17 – 4 pages

The story

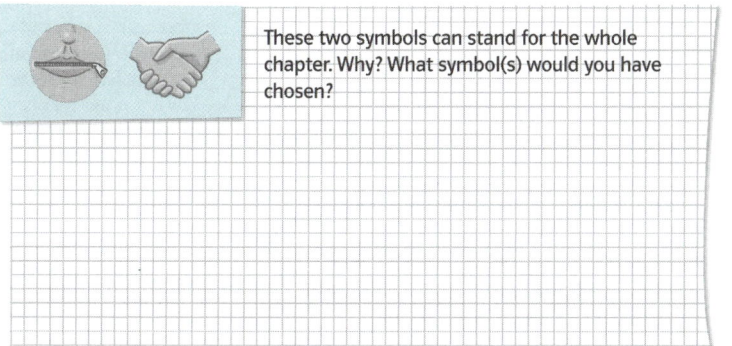

These two symbols can stand for the whole chapter. Why? What symbol(s) would you have chosen?

Here's a short summary of Chapter 17.
It's written in mirror image – can you decipher it?

Summary

Silas tries very hard
to make up
for his former wrongs,
but Larry stubbornly
refuses to talk to him.

1. Reading Guide

Quotes

Here are some key sentences from this chapter. Answer the questions.

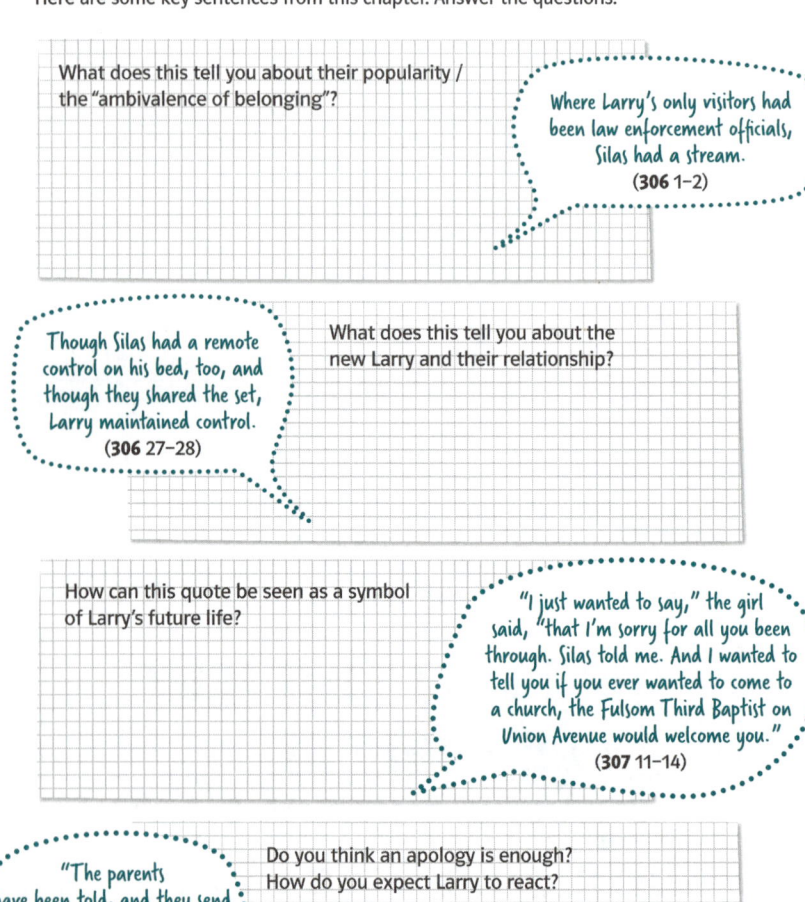

What does this tell you about their popularity / the "ambivalence of belonging"?

> Where Larry's only visitors had been law enforcement officials, Silas had a stream.
> (**306** 1–2)

> Though Silas had a remote control on his bed, too, and though they shared the set, Larry maintained control.
> (**306** 27–28)

What does this tell you about the new Larry and their relationship?

How can this quote be seen as a symbol of Larry's future life?

> "I just wanted to say," the girl said, "that I'm sorry for all you been through. Silas told me. And I wanted to tell you if you ever wanted to come to a church, the Fulsom Third Baptist on Union Avenue would welcome you."
> (**307** 11–14)

> "The parents have been told, and they send their apologies to Mr. Ott," nodding to Larry.
> (**309** 12–13)

Do you think an apology is enough? How do you expect Larry to react?

Vocab & Language

➢ Here are **eight words** from this chapter. What do they mean?
   Translate or explain.

apologize	
assure	
discharged	
ensue	
flush	
maintain control	
spiffy	
spot of blood	

➢ Note down expressions or phrases that you like and might want to recycle in
   your own writing:

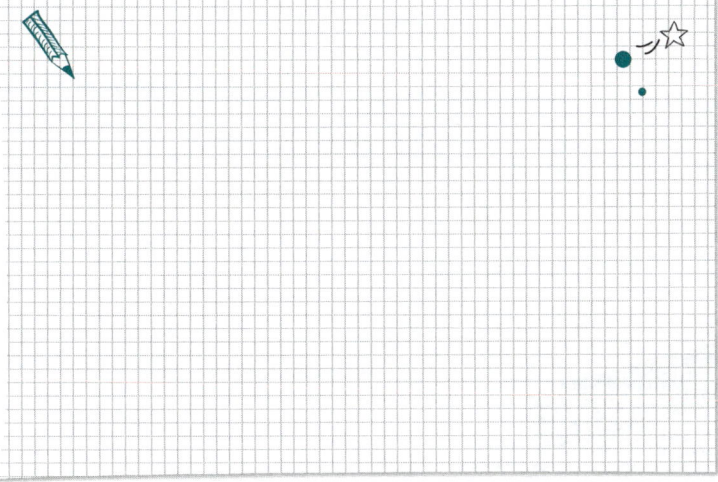

➤ Write down **three words** from the 4 pages that

are completely irrelevant to you:	you **like the sound of**:	you'd like **to remember**:
▶	▶	▶
▶	▶	▶
▶	▶	▶

Talk about it! Useful words to describe this chapter:

to refuse to do something   to stick to your opinion

Word field: stubborn

Which of these words do you know? Look up those you don't know and add some new words to the word field.

headstrong

adamant

obstinate

stubborn

uncompromising

pigheaded

Sneak Preview

These two symbols can represent the next chapter: What do you think will happen?

Focus is on: ☐ Larry ☐ Silas ☐ both

1.18   Chapter 18 – 5 pages

The story

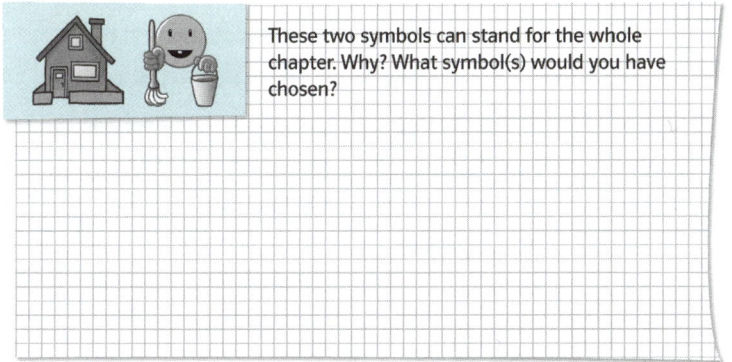

These two symbols can stand for the whole chapter. Why? What symbol(s) would you have chosen?

In this summary, four letters have been replaced by symbols.

Can you decipher the code?

Summary

Ȧngiȧ ȧnd ʕilȧʕ clȧȧn *p
Lȧrry'ʕ hoʕȧȧ ȧnd ʕȧt him *p to
bȧcomȧ pȧrt of thȧ comm*nity.

Ȧ = ...

ȧ = ...

* = ...

ʕ = ...

1. Reading Guide

 Quote

Read the following passage. What do you think the very last part of the sentence can refer to? Find some music to go with this scene.

> Holding it for a moment he was a boy again, the world the world it had been a long time ago, a world full of unknowns, a world full of future and possibility, but then he reached and set the rifle down stock first in the green velvet oval and fit its barrel in its green velvet groove and it stood there, a thing returned to its rightful place.
>
> (**314** 17–23)

Vocab & Language

➢ Here are **ten words and expressions** from these pages. What do they mean?
Translate or explain.

to baby someone	
chat	
decipher	
hum	
invincible	
penance	
pull into a parking lot	
reprimand	
squat	
velvet	

➢ Note down expressions or phrases that you like and might want to recycle in
your own writing:

Sneak Preview

Well, you've made it ... What follows is the final chapter.
Do you think all the conflicts and strands of the story can
be resolved in only seven pages?

1. Reading Guide

1.19   Chapter 19 – 7 pages

The story

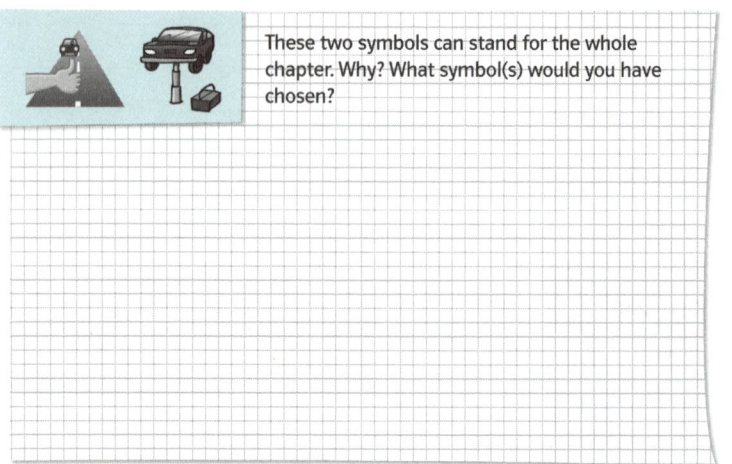

These two symbols can stand for the whole chapter. Why? What symbol(s) would you have chosen?

Here's a summary of the final chapter. Surely you can figure out what's wrong here?!

Summary

CAR SILAS' FIXING LARRY ABOUT AND ENGINES CAR ABOUT TALKING START MEN TWO THE WHEN RESTORED IS NORMALCY OF SENSE SOME FUTURE THEIR INTO GLIMPSE A GIVEN IS READER THE VISIBLE BARELY AND OVERGROWN IS NOW BY THAT HOUSE OLD WALKER'S THE PAST DRIVING HOME LIFT A HIM GIVES AND HIM FINDS SILAS REPORTERS THE AVOID TO NIGHT THE OF MIDDLE THE IN HOSPITAL THE LEAVES LARRY WHEN

Quote

The land had a way of covering the wrongs of people.

(**320** 29–30)

What do you think this sentence means?

Vocab & Language

➢ Here are the final **seven important words** from these pages.
What do they mean? Translate or explain.

anticipate	
bruised	
drench	
gift basket	
labor	
limp	
poke	

1. Reading Guide

Over to you

 How do you feel at the end of the chapter? How sentimental is the description of Larry's return?

Which were the scenes in the book that most moved you? Pick three.

1.20 In a nutshell

The front cover (or jacket)

Now that you have finished the novel, take another look at the cover.
Does it suit the story? Why / why not?

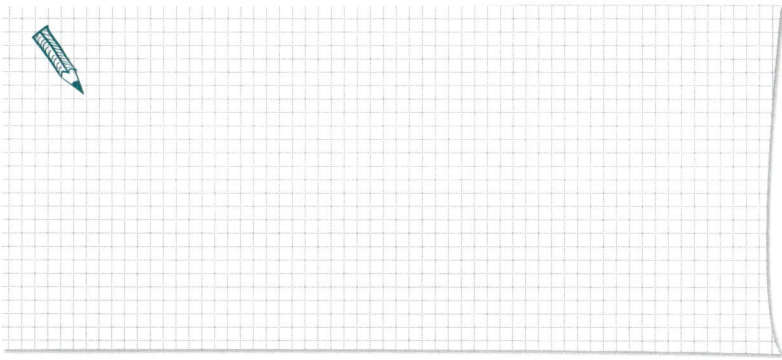

Stick an alternative cover here. This can be any picture
you would choose to go with the story.

1. Reading Guide

Over to you

 Pick five of the following sentence beginnings and complete them on the next pages. Ideally they'll nicely summarize your reading experience:

- This novel is not only about ...

- It is also about ...

- I especially liked the part (when / in which) ... because ...

- What I didn't particularly like was (when) ...

- The most exciting event was ...

- The passage I found particularly sad was ...

- The character I like best is ... because ....

- The sentence I will never forget is ... because ...

- If there were one thing I could change about the novel, I would ...

- What I don't understand is ...

- I would like to ask Tom Franklin ...

- ...

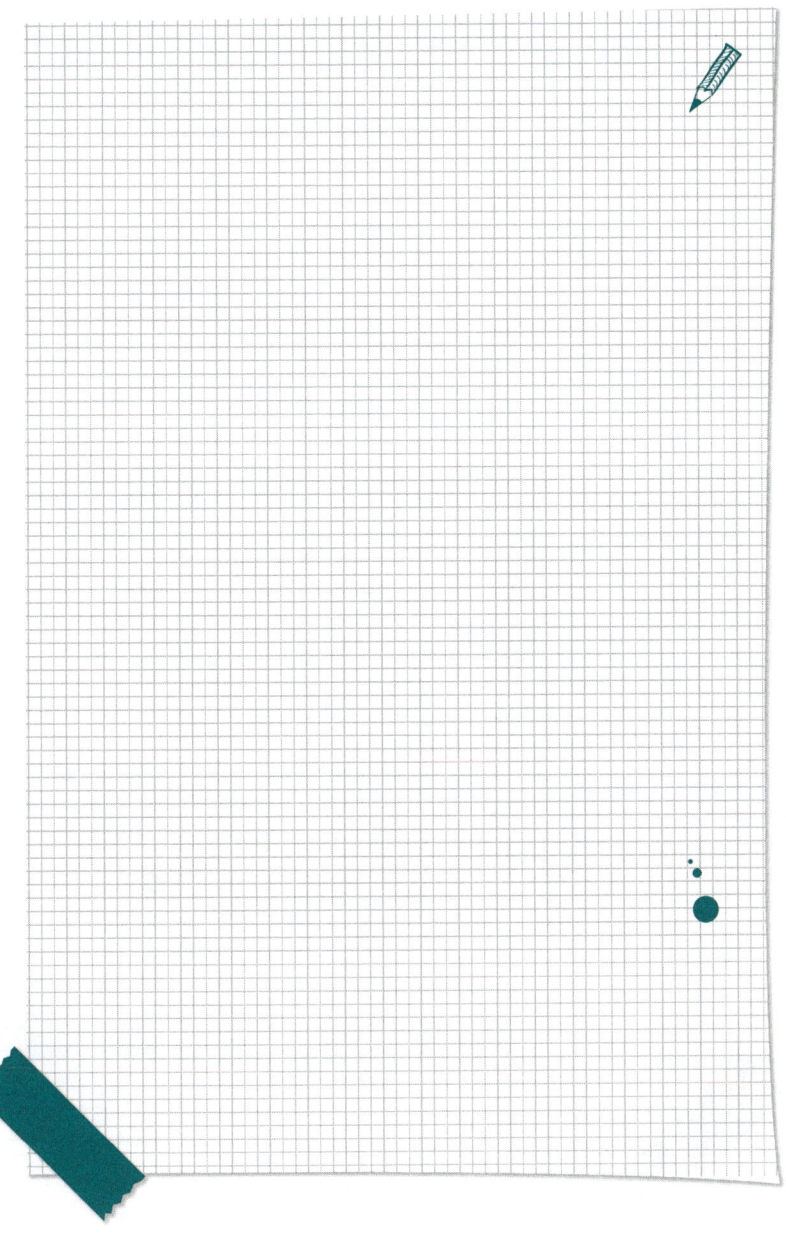

Plot-summary

Look at the symbols below. Retell the whole story by going from one symbol to another (you don't have to go in a straight line). Try to use all the symbols.

1. Reading Guide

Exam preparation

Go to page 326 of your book. Pick three of the 'Questions for discussion'. How would you answer them? Try to use some of the phrases and expressions you noted down in this journal.

Now that you've finished the novel write down five questions you would like to ask the author and / or characters from the novel. What do you think the answers might be?

2. Characters

2.1   Characterization

When writing a character description, consider the following aspects:

- Physical appearance: What does the person look like? (Try to draw a picture of the character or find a picture of what you think they look like.)
- Unique attributes: Do they have any personal quirks or habits? What is the first thing you'd notice about this person?
- Personal traits, talents, strengths and weaknesses
- Moral beliefs, likes and dislikes
- How do they interact with their environment?
- What do their immediate surroundings suggest about the person/their state of mind? Where do we meet them? What does this tell us about the person? Example: do we see them in an uncomfortable environment? If we get to know their home, what do we learn about their housekeeping skills etc.?
- How do they change throughout the story?

Remember to collect proof for your statements from the text. Use page and line references.

2.2   Useful vocab

When describing people, it obviously makes sense to use lots of adjectives. However, making use of adverbs and a variety of verbs and nouns will make any character description you write more interesting. Find and use synonyms (words that have a similar or the same meaning) to describe people.

Often, organizing your vocabulary helps. There's no single correct way of doing so: where one student might love **mind maps**, another will prefer **lists**, and yet another works best with **index cards**. You need to know what helps you and prepare your vocabulary accordingly.

The suggestions on the following pages are just that: suggestions, to be expanded or ignored – it's up to you.

Mind map: Appearance

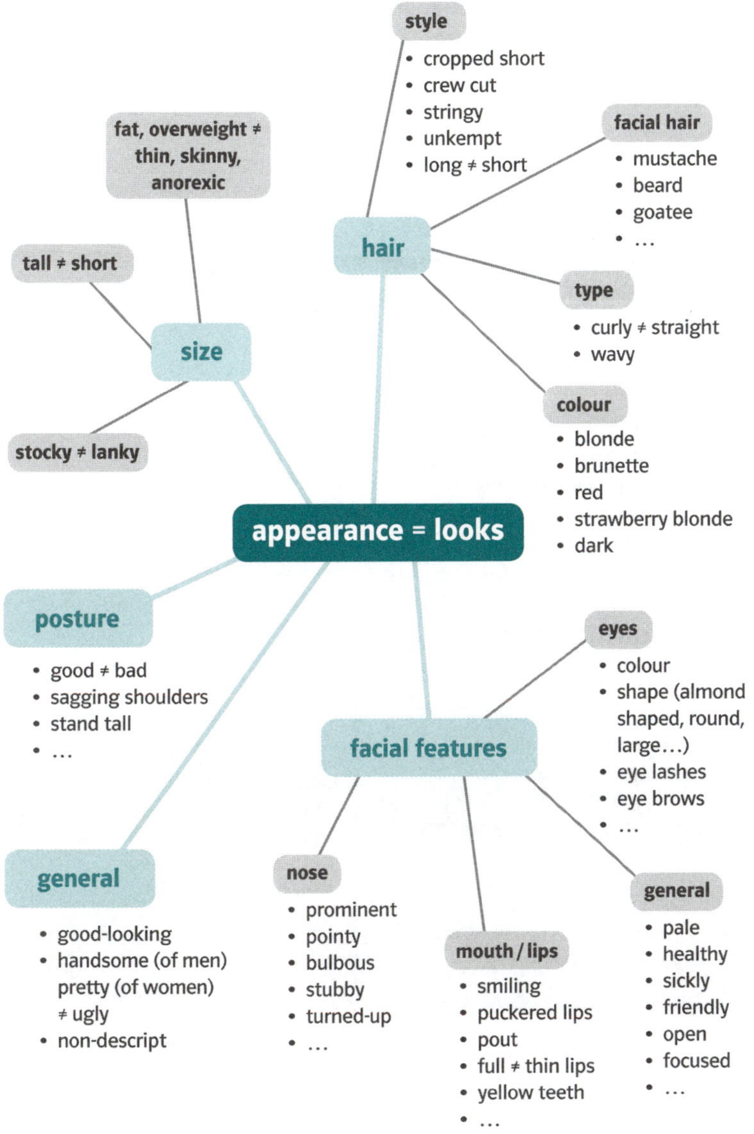

style
- cropped short
- crew cut
- stringy
- unkempt
- long ≠ short

facial hair
- mustache
- beard
- goatee
- …

fat, overweight ≠ thin, skinny, anorexic

tall ≠ short

hair

type
- curly ≠ straight
- wavy

size

colour
- blonde
- brunette
- red
- strawberry blonde
- dark

stocky ≠ lanky

appearance = looks

posture
- good ≠ bad
- sagging shoulders
- stand tall
- …

eyes
- colour
- shape (almond shaped, round, large…)
- eye lashes
- eye brows
- …

facial features

general
- good-looking
- handsome (of men) pretty (of women) ≠ ugly
- non-descript

nose
- prominent
- pointy
- bulbous
- stubby
- turned-up
- …

mouth / lips
- smiling
- puckered lips
- pout
- full ≠ thin lips
- yellow teeth
- …

general
- pale
- healthy
- sickly
- friendly
- open
- focused
- …

List: Habits

habit ['hæbɪt] = **custom or routine** *(An-)Gewohnheit* – sth you do regularly
a good / charming / bad / nasty habit *eine gute / reizende / schlechte / unangenehme Angewohnheit*

....

habit = **addiction** *Drogenabhängigkeit*
→ **to fund a habit** *eine Sucht finanzieren*
→ **to kick the habit** (informal) *von der Sucht loskommen*
habit-forming *süchtig machend*

....

habit = **tendency**
→ **to be in the habit of doing sth.**
habitual adj → *aus Gewohnheit*

Index cards: Ostracism

ostracism exclusion
to ostracise to exclude
to avoid sb intentionally or to exclude sb from becoming part of a group

After Cindy Walker had disappeared, Larry was ostracized by the local community.

ostracism Ächtung
to ostracise jdn ächten
to be ostracized ausgestoßen/ ausgeschlossen werden (von der Gesellschaft)

Words and phrases used in the novel to describe people

Jot down ones you like or find memorable while you read the novel!

2.3   Character profiles – Larry Ott

Complete Larry's pages.

Name: **Larry Ott**

What do you think he looks like? Find a picture and stick it here.

Appearance:

....

....

....

....

Family & home:

....

Job:

....

Friends:

....

....

....

Hobbies:

....

....

....

....

How does Larry see himself?

....

....

....

....

How do others see him?

....

....

....

....

2. Characters

Character profile – Silas Jones

Complete Silas' pages.

Name: Silas Jones

What do you think he looks like? Find a picture and stick it here.

Appearance:

....

....

....

....

Family & home:

....

Job:

....

Friends:

....

....

....

Hobbies:

....

....

....

....

How does Silas see himself?

....

....

....

....

How do others see him?

....

....

....

....

2. Characters

Character profile – Wallace Stringfellow

Complete Wallace's pages.

Name: **Wallace Stringfellow**

What do you think he looks like? Find a picture and stick it here.

Appearance:

....

....

....

....

Family & home:

....

Job:

....

Friends:

....

....

....

Hobbies:

....

....

....

....

How does Silas see himself?

....

....

....

....

How do others see him?

....

....

....

....

2. Characters

2.4   Relationships

Love

Note down who in the novel **loves** whom. Jot down at least one central quote.

Hate

Note down who in the novel **hates** whom. Why? Jot down at least one central quote.

3. Clues

While you read the novel, you will come across clues that help solve the four crimes. Because the author jumps back and forth between the past and the present it's not always easy to unravel the story. This section can help you to keep an overview.

Clues by chapter

Use this space to collect clues while reading the novel. Or – if you're a more organized person – add to the crime report files starting on p. 132 while you read.

Crime Report File: Case # 1

Victim: Cindy Walker, 16

Case overview:

Estimated time of crime:...

Crime scene:...

....

....

Suspect/s:...

....

Evidence:...

....

```
┌ ─ ─ ─ ─ ─ ─ ─ ─ ─ ─ ┐   ┌ ─ ─ ─ ─ ─ ─ ─ ─ ─ ─ ┐
│                     │   │                     │
│      Picture        │   │      Picture        │
│                     │   │                     │
└ ─ ─ ─ ─ ─ ─ ─ ─ ─ ─ ┘   └ ─ ─ ─ ─ ─ ─ ─ ─ ─ ─ ┘
```

Witnesses: ....
....

Relevant background information: ....
....

```
┌──────────────────────────────────────────────────┐
│ Conclusion:                                        │
│                                                    │
│                                                    │
│                                                    │
│                                                    │
│                                                    │
│                                                    │
│                                                    │
│                                                    │
│                                                    │
└──────────────────────────────────────────────────┘
```

Crime Report File: Case # 2

Victim: Tina Rutherford

Case overview:

Estimated time of crime:

Crime scene:

Suspect/s:

Evidence:

Witnesses: ....

....

Relevant background information: ....

....

Conclusion:

Crime Report File: Case # 3

Victim: Morton Morisette aka M&M

Case overview:

Estimated time of crime:...

Crime scene:...

....

....

Suspect/s:...

....

Evidence:...

....

```
Picture
```

```
Picture
```

Witnesses:...

....

Relevant background information:...

....

Conclusion:

Crime Report File: Case # 4

Victim: Larry Ott, 42

Case overview:

Estimated time of crime: ....

Crime scene: ....

....

....

Suspect/s: ....

....

Evidence: ....

....

Picture

Picture

Witnesses:..

....

Relevant background information:...

....

Conclusion:

4. Classroom Material

The following pages repeat copymasters your teacher might use in class. This is to save you all space and time. If you don't like this format much, you can go to www.klett-sprachen.de and enter the webcode **t6sp5hk** to access the material in A4 format and print it out.

Here's an overview of the copymasters *(Kopiervorlagen, KV)* printed here.

KV 2   The Language of the South
KV 4   Fitting in
KV 5   Defining "belonging"
KV 9   Larry's isolation
KV 14 A Reading Challenge
KV 18 Turning Points
KV 19 Story Telling – Larry and his father
KV 22 Guilt and redemption
KV 27 Chronology of events

A Reading Challenge

You might choose to ignore this section, but we do highly recommend that you at least look at **KV 14 A Reading Challenge** (pp.151–152).

A Note on Solutions

Your teacher has access to all the suggested solutions to the tasks on the following pages via the *Teacher's Guide* to the novel.

The Language of the South

The novel you're reading is set in the American South, in Mississippi.
There are many examples in the book where people use the local dialect or
adopt the way people speak in the South. This is often referred to as a
"Southern drawl". While you read, you should have the voices of the South in
your head and understand how people speak. The Internet (and especially
YouTube) is a great source of examples. To access the clips and information
referred to below, enter the **online code 5kgb2w4** into the search field on
www.klett-sprachen.de.

1. Watch your first lesson on YouTube:

"How to speak with a Southern Accent"

By the way, the Southern drawl has been voted
"the sexiest accent in America", used for example
by Texas native Matthew McConnaughey and
Louisiana-raised Britney Spears.

KV 2

⮕ While you listen, take notes on particular features:

Feel free to watch some more lessons and practise your own Southern drawl at home. Add more words or features to the list.

Word / expression	Meaning / difference

2. For a real impression of how people sound, watch (parts of) the interview with the musician Jerry Lee Lewis.

⮕ Choose one or two sentences the speakers use. Repeat them until you can get the pronunciation just right.

3. If you're interested in learning more about this accent, read up on the instructions taken from wikiHow:

   How to Develop a Southern Accent

   ⮕ What are the three methods mentioned?

Some of the language features are also listed in your book on pages 15 & 16.

Fitting in

Fitting in versus truly belonging – fitting in is NOT belonging:

> In fact, fitting in is the greatest barrier to belonging. Fitting in, I've discovered during the past decade of research, is assessing situations and groups of people, then twisting yourself into a human pretzel in order to get them to let you hang out with them. Belonging is something else entirely—it's showing up and letting yourself be seen and known as you really are—love of gourd painting, intense fear of public speaking and all. Many of us suffer from this split between who we are and who we present to the world in order to be accepted.
>
> Brené Brown, American scholar and author

1. Read the following scenarios. On your own, tick the appropriate box
   – which would be the most likely reaction or decision for you personally?

Scenario 1

Someone has played a prank on you that embarrasses you in public and everyone is laughing at you. How do you react?

☐ a) Laugh along with the crowd. You love a good joke even if it's at your expense.

☐ b) You pretend to laugh along because you don't want anyone to know that they really hurt your feelings by making you look stupid in front of everybody else.

☐ c) You get upset and run away from the crowd. How could they be so mean?

☐ d) What a jerk! You get mad and tell them what you think right there and then.

☐ e) You pretend that all is well, but you won't forget this. They're going to pay for what they did! How dare they humiliate you in public?

Scenario 2

A friend of yours tells you that there is some really cool stuff in an old abandoned building. When you get there you see a sign that says "Danger: Do not enter!", but the building doesn't look dangerous. There is nobody around to see you and your friend wants to check it out.

- [ ] a) Obviously there is some dangerous stuff in there and we shouldn't be going inside.
- [ ] b) Maybe I'll just take a quick peek. It won't hurt!
- [ ] c) To hell with the danger! There's probably some cool stuff inside. Let's see what all the fuss is about.

Scenario 3

You have just returned home from a long day's work when an acquaintance calls you and explains that their car has broken down on a side road an hour's drive from town and they're asking you to pick them up. They've already tried everyone else and you are their only means of getting back. What do you do or say?

- [ ] a) I'm too tired. I tell them to try to flag down a car to help them out.
- [ ] b) I make up a lie about why I can't help them.
- [ ] c) I'll do it, but I'll charge them for gas money.
- [ ] d) Yes, I'm tired, but what are friends for?
- [ ] e) I ask them what's wrong with the car. Maybe I can talk them through how to fix it.

Scenario 4

Five years ago some classmates stole some money from you but never got into trouble for it. Since then, they have become much better people. Recently, they have been arrested for stealing, but you can prove that they are innocent.

- [ ] a) I won't say anything. This is the punishment that they never got five years ago.

- [ ] b) I'll tell them that I'll save them, provided they pay me back the money they owe me.

- [ ] c) I'll save them because I know they are much better people now.

- [ ] d) I'll save them even if they havn't changed because I know they are innocent this time.

2. Work with a partner. Pick one scenario each and ask your partner to explain which decision they came to, and why. What would the consequences of your decision be? What do your results say about you as a person?

3. Relate your findings to the novel. With your partner, go through each scenario again and try and answer a) as Larry might have done, and b) as Silas might have done.

4. Make up one more scenario together that you feel goes with the novel and Larry's desire to fit in and belong to some peer group. Then discuss your scenario with another pair.

5. In class, discuss the following statement:

   „As social animals, we humans are ultimately driven by one motive only – our hunger to belong!" Collect arguments for and against this statement.

Homework: Write a composition using the arguments from above.

KV 5

Definitions

Read the following definitions (A – G).

1. One sentence has been taken out of every definition, as marked by [...].
   Choose the correct sentence (1 – 8) from the following page to complete
   each text. There is one sentence that you don't need.

2. Work with a partner. For each definition, choose an appropriate example
   from the novel. If you have also worked with the film *Gran Torino*, you
   might like to add some more examples, perhaps in a different color.

A The **need to belong**, also often referred to as **belongingness**, refers to a human
emotional need to affiliate with and be accepted by members of a group. [....]
It involves more than simply being acquainted with other people. It is instead
centered on gaining acceptance, attention and support from members of the
group as well as providing the same attention to other members.

B Ostracism
The social psychologist Kipling Williams has written extensively on ostracism as
a modern phenomenon. Williams defines ostracism as "any act or acts of
ignoring and excluding of an individual or groups by an individual or a group".
Williams suggests that the most common form of ostracism in a modern
context is refusing to communicate with a person. [....] Williams and his
colleagues have charted responses to ostracism in some five thousand cases,
and found two distinctive patterns of response. The first is increased group-
conformity, in a quest for re-admittance; the second is to become more
provocative and hostile to the group, seeking attention rather than acceptance.

C Social isolation is a state of complete or near-complete lack of contact
between an individual and society. It differs from loneliness, which reflects a
temporary lack of contact with other humans. [....] It might also include having
no communication with family, acquaintances or friends, and/or willfully
avoiding any contact with other humans when those opportunities do arise.

D Loneliness is a complex and usually unpleasant emotional response to isolation. Loneliness typically includes anxious feelings about a lack of connection or communication with other beings, both in the present and extending into the future. As such, loneliness can be felt even when surrounded by other people. The causes of loneliness are varied and include social, mental, emotional, or even physical factors. Research has shown that loneliness is prevalent throughout society, including people in marriages, relationships, families, veterans, and those with successful careers. It has been a long explored theme in the literature of human beings since classical antiquity. Loneliness has also been described as social pain—a psychological mechanism meant to motivate an individual to seek social connections. Loneliness is often defined in terms of one's connectedness to others. [….]

E Bullying is the use of force, threat, or coercion to abuse, intimidate or aggressively dominate others. [….] One essential prerequisite is the perception, by the bully or by others, of an imbalance of social or physical power, which distinguishes bullying from conflict. Behaviors used to assert such domination can include verbal harassment or threat, physical assault or coercion, and such acts may be directed repeatedly towards particular targets. If bullying is done by a group, it is called mobbing.

F Social integration is a dynamic and structured process in which all members participate in a dialogue to achieve and maintain peaceful social relations. Social integration does not mean forced assimilation. Social integration is focused on the need to move toward a safe, stable and just society. [….] and by expanding and strengthening conditions of social integration — towards peaceful social relations of coexistence, collaboration and cohesion.

G Humiliation is the abasement of pride, which leads to a state of being humbled or reduced to lowliness or submission. It is an emotion felt by a person whose social status has just decreased. [….] The loss of status, like losing a job or being labeled as a liar or discredited unfairly, could cause people's inability to behave normally in their communities. Humiliated individuals could be provoked and crave for revenge, and some people could feel worthless, hopeless and helpless, creating suicidal thoughts if justice is not met.

4. Classroom Material

What definition do these sentences complete?

Definition

✂

---

1 All types of social isolation can include staying home for lengthy periods of time.

5 It is a judgment of oneself as well as an attitude toward the self. Thus, it encompasses beliefs about oneself, (for example, "I am competent", "I am worthy"), as well as emotional states, such as triumph, despair, pride, and shame.

---

2 It has been called "the unpleasant experience that occurs when a person's network of social relations is deficient in some important way."

6 It is aimed at mending conditions of social disintegration and social exclusion—social fragmentation, exclusion and polarization

---

3 It can be brought about through intimidation, physical or mental mistreatment or trickery, or by embarrassment if a person is revealed to have committed a socially or legally unacceptable act or acts.

7 The behavior is often repeated and habitual.

---

4 By refusing to communicate with a person, that person is effectively ignored and excluded.

8 This may include the need to belong to a peer group at school, to be accepted by co-workers, to be part of an athletic team or to be part of a church group.

Examples from the novel:

Larry's isolation

1. Larry Ott is a very lonely man. With a partner, brainstorm your ideas on factors that you feel have contributed to his isolation.

2. Look at the table below. Parts of it have already been done for you. Complete the grid.

Key word/factor	Example from the text/key event
Name	Larry is "odd" if you pronounce his name with an American accent; "Larry" doesn't sound like very much.
	Larry suffers from asthma attacks as a child. He can't play with other kids.
Language	
	He feels he has no skills as a mechanic or cannot cut the grass.
Sports	
Masculinity	
	Larry reads a lot of books and withdraws into an alternative world.
Technology	Equipment in the garage and his house (remote control, TV etc.).
	The date – he becomes the main suspect in a murder investigation.
Father	
	He is one of the few white kids at his school.
Mask	
	His mother becomes ill and sometimes doesn't even recognize him. He has no-one to talk to.
The garage	There are fewer and fewer customers, resulting in his having even fewer contacts with the outside world.

KV 9

3. **Discuss:** Which of these factors came first, which developed later? Is it possible to establish a time line? Which factors resulted in yet another factor / his growing isolation?

4. Use the key words from the first column to **create a graphic representation** of Larry's isolation.
   Use a separate sheet, please. You can choose the shapes or symbols you want to use yourself.

5. Distribute your graphs or drawings around the room and have a vernissage. Explain your graphic representation and your reasons for choosing this particular shape.
   Sum up your findings in no more than 40 words:

Larry becomes isolated because ....

A reading challenge

This novel has over 300 pages. It will be a real challenge to get to grips with such a long book in another language. Need some incentives? Here are some ideas for you:

1. Try and tick all of the following options.

   ☐ I read the book in bed.

   ☐ I read the book on a bus/train/my way to school.

   ☐ I read some pages in the dark using a flashlight.

   ☐ I read a chapter sitting at my desk.

   ☐ I read some pages aloud to a friend.

   ☐ I read a chapter together with a friend.

   ☐ I read while the sun was shining.

   ☐ I read some pages before 6 am.

   ☐ I read a few pages after 11 pm.

   ☐ I read one page upside down.

   ☐ I read some pages in my pyjamas.

   ☐ I read a few pages in the bathtub.

2. Find a **reading buddy** in class – someone who can help you (and whom you will help) to get through the book.

   My reading buddy is: ....

a) After every chapter, text each other and exchange emoticons: find 10–15 emoticons that you find relevant for the plot or what you remember most about the story. Try and re-tell the story to yourself using your partner's emoticons. **Or:**

b) Send **one** single picture to your reading buddy after every chapter that you have finished. The picture can be anything, but should be something you associate with the events in the chapter. Can your partner guess what is being depicted here or what you meant by your picture?
Once you have finished the novel, look at all the pictures once again. Can you piece the storyline together just by looking at what your buddy sent you/what you sent them?

Reading progress: Color the bar every time you finish reading a chapter (or significant parts of it). The size of the boxes represents the length of the chapters.

1	2	3	4	5	6	7	8	9	10	11	12	13	14	15	16	17	18	19

KV 14

3. Time yourself

Read the first chapter using an alarm clock.

It took me .... minutes to read pp. 17–25.

Multiply this time by 36. This is your personal estimated reading time for *Crooked Letter, Crooked Letter*. Don't despair! The novel has many interesting episodes and loads of murders and cliff-hangers, so you won't get bored (once you've made it past Chapter 2…).

Color in the bar at the edge of this page for every chapter you have completed. You can check the total reading time that remains.

You might also like to check www.readinglength.com. They reckon that the average reading time for *Crooked Letter, Crooked Letter* is 6 hours and 16 minutes, if you read about 250 words per minute (wpm).

There are about 12 words per line, 32 lines per page. That's roughly 380 words per page for this edition. If you can manage half a page in one minute, you have an average reading time of 190 wpm. That means you can read this in around 8 hours 16. Reading just 30 minutes a day means you can get it done in 2 weeks.

KV 18

Turning points

In every story or novel there are a number of turning points where things could have gone differently.

Step 1: With a partner, choose one event from each of your lives. Talk about what happened. How might things have developed differently?

Example:

If my parents hadn't moved to Stuttgart, I would have been born in Cologne.
If I had been born in Cologne, I wouldn't go to this school.
If I went to another school, I wouldn't have met you.

Step 2: Look at the following examples of possible turning points from the novel.

a) Match the two parts.

b) Write your own sentences as you continue reading
Crooked Letter, Crooked Letter.

1. If Larry hadn't taught Silas how to use a gun,	a) she would perhaps still be alive.
2. If Cindy Walker hadn't been in the habit of sunbathing,	b) he might not have become a policeman.
3. If Silas' mum hadn't had sex with Carl,	c) the two might never have become lovers.
4. If they hadn't returned to Chabot,	d) Silas would not have grown up in Chicago.
5. If Silas' mother hadn't left Mississippi,	e) Silas and Larry would never have met.
6. If Silas hadn't taken the snake out of the letterbox,	f) she wouldn't have become pregnant.
7. If Larry hadn't taken Silas to watch Cindy Walker,	g) they wouldn't have laid so many eggs.
8. If Larry hadn't looked after the chickens so well,	h) someone would have died.

Step 3: Arguably, the biggest turning point in the novel is Larry's date with Cindy Walker. Before you work on the following section, please re-read pp. 158–168. Then tick the correct boxes:

True or false? – Consider these statements.	true	false
Cecil Walker is extremely violent to Larry and extremely rude to Cindy.	☒	☐
Cindy is happy about the beer that Larry gives her.	☐	☒
Larry misunderstands Cindy when she says "scootch over".	☒	☐
Both Cecil and Larry claim that Cindy is safe with them.	☒	☐
Cindy gives Larry only a very rough idea of what he needs to do that evening.	☐	☒

Complete this sentence.

At the movie, Larry realizes that Ken and David _are behind him_

and decides _to put a blanket around his_
hand

Step 5: Tick the correct answer(s). More than one answer may be correct.

While Cindy drives his car,

a ☒ Larry is afraid his father will be angry.

b ☒ she drinks beer, smokes and listens to the Bee Gees.

c ☒ he can see far up her legs.

d ☐ she talks about Cecil all the time.

154

At the drive-in,	a	☒	Larry parks almost at the back.
	b	☒	Ken and David follow him.
	c	☐	Larry doesn't play along with Cindy's plan.
	d	☒	Larry uses a clever trick to pretend Cindy is with him.

While he waits for Cindy to come back,	a	☐	he ironically listens to the song "Staying Alive".
	b	☐	he clearly shows his frustration about this disaster of a date.
	c	☒	he waits for over 90 minutes before he gets all worked up.
	d	☒	Larry tries to calm himself down again and again.

What would you have done? Take 2–3 minutes to jot down some ideas from Larry's point of view.
Then discuss in class: Do you feel Larry should have refused to play along? Why did he go through with the sham?

KV 19

Storytelling – Larry and his father

In an interview, Tom Franklin talks about storytelling and how he realized as a child that a story starts taking on a life of its own if it's told again and again.

Let's take a closer look at how his experience found its way into *Crooked Letter, Crooked Letter*.

1. Re-read pp. 64 l. 11 – 66 l. 5.

2. Draw a rough picture of the scene at the garage. Pay particular attention to where you imagine Larry is in relation to his father.

3. If Larry could put the experience of listening to his father in a nutshell, what would he say? Write one sentence only. Start like this:

   I simply loved listening to his stories because ....

   ....

   ....

4. Discuss: Is Larry in any way like his father? How good is he at storytelling himself?

5. Draw a cartoon version of the story that Carl tells his friends. Use three pictures only. Jot down some words to jog your memory. To what extent do you think the story is racist? Try and retell the story using your drawings as a guideline.

Homework: Watch an episode from the film *Stand by me* by Rob Reiner.

You can find it on YouTube by looking for "The pie eating contest" or by entering the **online code czhvkyt** in the search field on www.klett-sprachen.de. You can also scan the QR code.

czhvkyt

In this scene, one of the teenagers is good at storytelling and spins an incredible yarn. Watch the episode twice. Which words or phrases can you use or recycle when you tell a story yourself?

Practise storytelling on your own. Can you retell the whole story?

KV 22

Guilt and redemption – The new Silas

1. Match the following definitions with the appropriate word.

atonement   empathy   guilt   redemption   remorse
retribution   selfishness

a) Having or showing concern only for oneself, seeking or concentrating on one's own pleasure, advantage, or well-being, without regard for others.

b) Reparation for an offense or injury.

c) The feeling that you under-stand and share another person's experiences and emotions.

d) A bad feeling caused by knowing or thinking that you have done something bad or wrong, have committed a breach of conduct, especially when violating the law and involving a penalty.

e) Something that is done or given as a way of correcting a mistake that you have made or a bad situation that you have caused. The act of making amends.

f) The act of making something better or more acceptable. In religious terms, the act of saving people from sin and evil.

g) Feeling sorry for doing something bad or wrong in the past; a feeling of guilt.

Guilt and redemption – The new Silas

2. With a partner, talk about the role of guilt in your lives. Discuss:
   - Is guilt just a religious concept?
   - What do people usually feel guilty about?
   - What can people do to overcome their feelings of guilt?
   - What would society be like if there was no such thing as guilt?

3. Use **two different colors** to mark the following statements about Silas: one color for true and one for false statements. Correct the false statements

   ☐ After Cindy Walker disappears, he keeps worrying about her.

   ☐ Although he worries about what his colleagues might think, Silas knows that the chickens would die without his help, so he feeds them and even buys more food for them.

   ☐ Silas asks Angie to help him to clean up Larry's place: they get rid of the blood stains and even install a satellite dish.

   ☐ Silas goes and visits Larry's mother in the nursing home because he wants to find out more about his past.

   ☐ Silas is more interested in finding a friend than in borrowing the rifle.

   ☐ Silas realizes that he needs to talk to Larry about their past and that they have to make a new start.

   ☐ When he lives in the cabin with his mom and the cat disappears, he keeps nagging his mother about the cat's whereabouts.

   ☐ When Larry asks him about the nature of their relationship, he finds it easy to use the word friendship.

   ☐ When Larry gets bullied at school, Silas is always by his side and supports him.

   ☐ When Larry is in a coma, Silas visits him in hospital and whispers into his ear not to confess.

   ☐ When Larry leaves the hospital and tries to walk home, Silas follows him and offers him a ride.

   ☐ When people ask, Silas tells everyone about their friendship.

4. Now look at the two categories that have emerged by using two different colors. Find a common denominator to sum up what your two colors stand for.

   ☐ stands for .... ☐ stands for ....

5. Explain the quote on page 305 in this context:
   "With such gaps in his understanding, he saw very clearly how the boy he'd been had grown to be the man he was."

6. How would you personally characterize Silas' development throughout the novel?

KV 27

Chronology of events

On the following pages, you will find various pictures supposedly taken from the family albums of Silas Jones and Larry Ott. A color version is available online. Enter the code **6nqsqmh** into the searchfield on www.klett-sprachen.de or scan the QR-Code.

6nqsqmh

1. Use these pictures to retell the story.
2. With a partner, discuss the chronology of events from the beginning to the end. Put numbers next to the pictures. You can, of course, also cut out the pictures and put them back together again in a chronological order.
3. Which additional pictures would you have chosen to fill the gaps in the chronology?

I. Silas Jones

II. Larry Ott

Chapter 1

Quotes

What is implied about Larry in these quotes?

Larry had always felt bad that the hens lived their lives in the same tiny patch …. (**19** 1–2)

"You're what we call a person of interest." (**22** 27)

„Die," he said again. Okay with Larry. (**25** 5)

Chapter 2

The story

Put these events into the order they are mentioned in (in Chapter 2).

Description of "white trash Avenue", the part of town no-one wants to live in. ○

He doesn't have a lot of friends outside his work. ○

People don't go to Larry's garage. ○

Silas and M&M go back a long way. Silas is not very good at keeping in touch. ○

Silas doesn't want to revive the friendship to Larry. ○

Silas is about to discover a dead body. ○

Silas knows Larry. Larry knows about animals. ○

Silas recognizes the piece of clothing, i.e. he knows the dead man. ○

Silas' girlfriend is introduced. ○

The locals all ostracize Larry. If someone waves back, they only do so because they don't know about Larry or his "history". ○

We know Tina has disappeared – will the buzzards lead Silas to her body? ①

Chapter 3

Quotes

While you read, find quotes in the novel illustrating the following:

They're either poor or new to the area. Larry is very observant.

your choice

Larry feels uncomfortable around black kids.

your choice

He notices how his mother's mood changes. He realizes he shouldn't have told her.

your choice

Larry observes Carl and his admiring friends. He's not part of the crowd.

your choice

Detailed description of how he watches (almost stalks) Cindy.

your choice

Larry realizes that David and Ken are up to something but he's desperate to be accepted.

your choice

Larry had hoped that he would be accepted and get more support from the white kids, but they still laugh at him.

your choice

A subtle hint that maybe Carl gave Alice a car since he can no longer give them a lift after Ina's intervention.

your choice

Larry is kind and caring. He'd do anything for this friendship.

your choice

Chapter 4

Clues

 We are also given these clues in this chapter. What do you as a detective
make of them? Take some notes:

The Stephen King books:

Silas doesn't return the phone call:

Quotes

A frozen in the 1960s kind of character.

(**91** 24)

Explain: what does French mean?

5. Digging Deeper

Your views

 Speculate: how will the story continue?

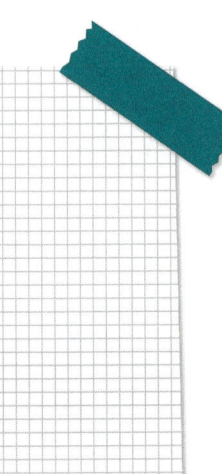

Imagine you were Silas walking through Larry's house: how would you feel?
What can you see / hear / smell / taste?

Chapter 5

Quotes

Match the passages given on the left to the short summary on the right.

98 5–6	Larry secretly thinks about the strange relationship between his dad and Silas' mum.
99 21–22	Silas doesn't like snakes.
100 12–15	Alice doesn't want her son to befriend Larry. Larry thinks it's a question of race, but the true reason is revealed later.
101 9–10	Cecil is mean and dangerous.
102 7–8	Silas is critical of Larry's passiveness.
106 9–10	Ina has had enough.
111 5–11	Carl hates it when Larry reads too much.
113 12–13	Ina cares a lot for Larry. Larry isn't very healthy.
116 33–34	Carl is a heavy drinker.

Chapter 6

Quotes

Find a sentence that you think is essential to this chapter. Why?

Chapter 7

Quotes

Reread these lines. Why might they be relevant?

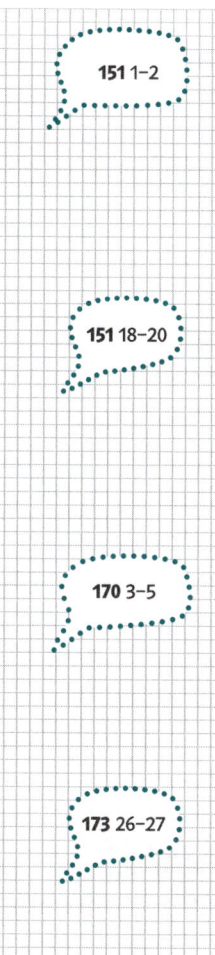

151 1–2

151 18–20

170 3–5

173 26–27

Over to you

Listen to *Hazard* by Richard Marx. Google the lyrics and find similarities and differences between the song and the two girls gone missing in the novel.

Similarities	Differences

Chapter 8

Characters

Why doesn't Silas tell Angie the truth? Come up with possible reasons in an angel – devil conversation. Start like this:

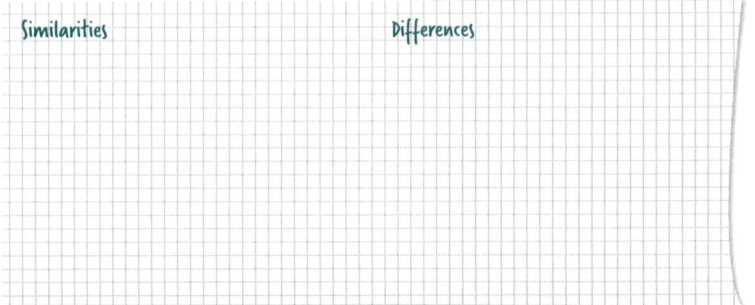

Tell her, Silas. You'll feel so much better.

Yes, but if you tell her, she'll know that you trust her.

No, don't tell her, Silas. She'll hate you if she ever finds out what you did to Larry.

Chapter 9

Friendship

Friendship plays an important role in the whole field of 'belonging'. Compare Larry's and Wallace's friendship with the boyhood friendship between Larry and Silas. How do these friendships develop? Find similarities and differences.

	Larry & Silas	Larry & Wallace
Similarities		
Differences		

Chapter 10

Post-reading

After reading this chapter, come up with **five** questions you would like to ask the author and / or characters from the novel at this stage.

Chapter 11

Post-reading

How do the two policemen try to get a confession out of Larry.

Chapter 12

Friendship

How does the author depict the encounter between Silas and Larry?
What are your personal FEELINGS while reading?

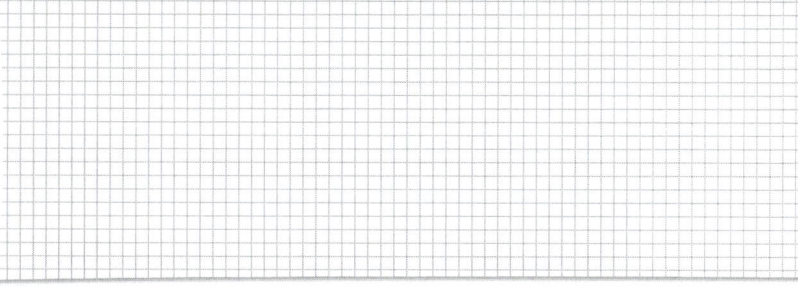

 Characters

What you think about **Chief French** so far? Is he a nice character or a nasty one? Why?

5. Digging Deeper

What you think about **Wallace Stringfellow**? Nice or nasty? Why?

Chapter 13

over to you

In this chapter, Larry keeps changing TV channels all the time. Why do you think he does this? What effect does this have on you as the reader?

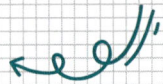

Chapter 14

Over to you

What do you think a cartoon version of the climax in this chapter could look like? Outline or draw one scene only. Don't forget to include the final piece of the puzzle: Larry's mask.

5. Digging Deeper

Chapter 15

Quotes

The passages referred to below can be seen as examples for symbolism and humor. Which is which and why?

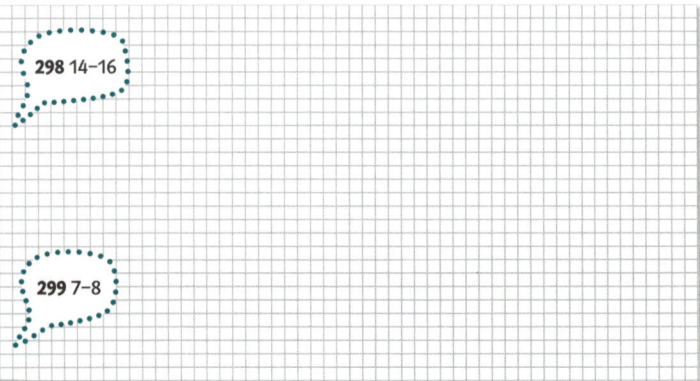

At the very end of chapter 15, Larry is lost in thought. What might have been different, if…?

"And what if he'd told Silas what he knew when Silas had asked him? Would the outcome have been different?"

(300 21–22)

Jot down your ideas of how things might have worked out differently.

Chapter 16

Language in use

Briefly outline the story the anchorwoman is reporting. How does the style of language differ from the rest of the narration?

Chapter 17

Comic relief

At the end of this chapter, there is some comic relief when Larry doesn't want to move out of his room. Can you think of three other examples of humor in the novel, perhaps a scene that made you smile?

comic relief a stylistic device where sth humorous or funny is inserted into a dramatic or serious scene to relieve the tension

Chapter 18

The story

Complete the following sentence:

Cleaning Larry's house means that ….

It stands for the idea of ….

 Over to you

What do you think Silas told the reporter?

How does Larry react to Silas' attempts at making conversation?
How would you have reacted?

314 17–23

What are some of the unknowns in Silas' life? Your life?
What future lies ahead?

Chapter 19

Setting

What does this short passage tell you about Fulsom? Do you remember similar passages from earlier on in the novel?

> They passed through the quiet Fulsom town square, the hardware store now a tanning salon slash manicure-pedicure joint. The drugstore a video rental place with a going-out-of-business sign in the window. Two closed barbershops, their poles plastered with stickers and graffiti. A block east, centered in a streetlight, a bent dog was eating something in the middle of the road and backed up as they passed. A box of chicken.
>
> (**319** 30 – **320** 2)

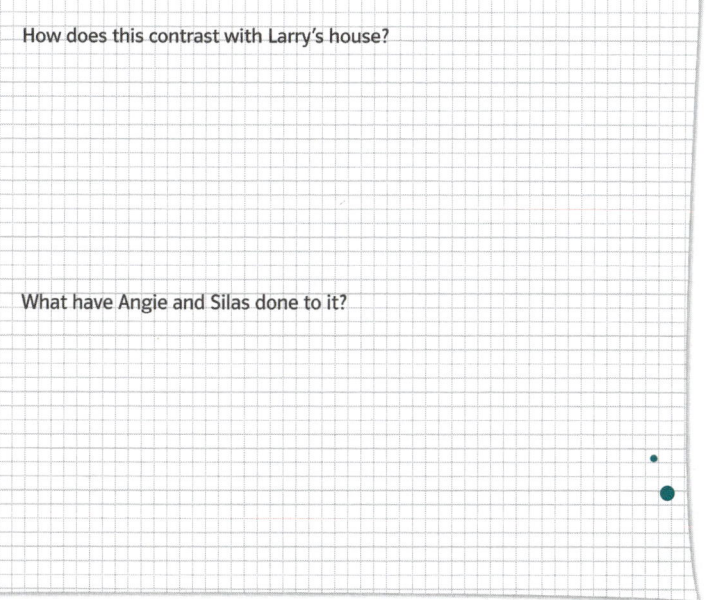

How does this contrast with Larry's house?

What have Angie and Silas done to it?

Stuff you want to remember for your exam / Abi

6. Your Notes

7. Solutions of sorts

Remember – this is **your** reading journal. Your thoughts and ideas matter!
Where useful, we've added suggestions to tasks, but we're not spoon-feeding
you everything...

1 Reading journal

1.1

This chapter focuses on: Larry

The story – Summary: solution available via Augmented App.
(1.1 Summary – solution)

Quotes: suggested solutions available via Augmented App.
(1.1 Quotes – meaning and 1.1 More quotes – meaning)

Quote in context: (**23** 30 – **24** 3)

- This is the cliffhanger at the end of Chapter 1.
- The protagonist we've been introduced to gets shot.
- The reader becomes curious and wants to find out more.
- Clue: Larry might know his assassin ($\rightarrow$ "something familiar").
- The passage also links the disappearance of two missing girls.
- The chapter spans 25 years.

1.2

This chapter focuses on: Silas

The story – Summary: We meet Silas, police constable in Chabot, Mississippi.
His nickname is 32, his number when he played baseball. Silas is rather popular,
black and he likes sports. Seemingly he is the complete opposite to Larry Ott.
He searches for Tina Rutherford, the daughter of the local mill owner. Alarmed
by a flock of birds, he decides to investigate and finds a corpse in the process.
Lying in the swamp, bloated and half-eaten, is M&M, an old school acquaintance
and local drug dealer. The police constable also helps Irina, an attractive young
woman who keeps flirting with him, to remove a snake from her mailbox.
Following Silas' instructions, his girlfriend Angie finds Larry injured and
unconscious in his house.

Quotes: suggested solutions available via Augmented App.
(1.2 Quotes – meaning and 1.2 More quotes – meaning)

Clues and **Over to you:** For these types of questions, there is no right or wrong. You decide what you find relevant. But make sure you can argue your point!

1.3

This chapter focuses on: Larry

The story – Summary: Larry meets Silas for the first time when his father Carl gives him and his mother Alice a ride into town in the freezing cold. The two adults seem to know each other. Larry befriends Silas and we learn that both like to go out into nature where they practice shooting in the woods – squirrels being their main target. Larry lends Silas a rifle and is amazed that Silas wants to keep all the cartridges. The relationship between Carl and Larry is difficult. Carl feels his son is "mechanically disinclined". Larry, who is one of the few white students at school, is very clumsy when it comes to "boy-ish" things. Trying to fit in, he allows David and Ken to egg him on and calls a black girl "monkey lips", which totally backfires and increases his isolation. Larry has a crush on Cindy Walker and watches her from a distance.

Quotes: suggested solutions available via Augmented App.
(1.3 Quotes – meaning and 1.3 More quotes – meaning)

Talk about it! words or expressions you might have added: an outside observer; watching people; spying on people; father-son relationship; gifts; presents; donations

1.4

This chapter focuses on: Silas

The story – Summary: After speaking to Angie, **Silas** finds out that **Larry** has been taken to hospital and is in a **coma**. He drives out to Larry's house and **looks around**, investigating living quarters and the **barn**. Silas is impressed with how **neat** the place is. He **realizes** that Larry has become isolated and **lonely** with only his **books** and **chickens** as **companions**. Remembering his boyhood and their **friendship**, he moves from room to room **but** finds nothing unusual. Chief French arrives and they talk about Larry's strangeness. They wonder about the **beer** in Larry's fridge and about the **gun** that he was not allowed to own. When Silas **gets** home, there is a short important **message** from Larry on his **answering machine**.

Quotes: suggested solutions available via Augmented App.
(1.4 Quotes – meaning)

7. Solutions of sorts

1.5

This chapter focuses on: Larry and Silas

The story – Summary: 1. T; 2. F (Larry is relieved when Carl says no. He has other plans.); 3. T; 4. F (Silas keeps away from snakes, Larry says he's no good at baseball.); 5. T; 6. T; 7.T; 8. F (Silas helps Cindy whereas Larry cannot spring into action.); 9. F (He forces them into a nasty and cruel fight.); 10. T

Quotes: suggested solutions available via Augmented App.
(1.5 Quotes – meaning and 1.5 More quotes – meaning)

Vocab & Language: to work together, to collaborate: **to team up on**; to not succeed, to disappoint the expectations or trust of: **to fail**; to attack by surprise from a hidden place: **ambush**; a removable covering for a pillow: **pillowcase**; to exchange: **to trade**; the space between a woman's breasts: **cleavage**; to live in a building or on land without the owner's permission and without paying: **to squat**; acting too quickly, eager, impatient: **hasty**; suitable for girls but not for boys; having the qualities of a girl: **girly**; intensity, violence: **fierceness**

1.6

This chapter focuses on: Silas

The story – Summary: Listen to the correct order via the Augmented App.
(1.6 Summary)

1. Silas talks to Miss Marla…; 2. First, he finds some small pieces …;
3. When he picks up …; 4 Finally, he tries to …; 5. In the barn, he …;
6. Back inside the house …; 7. Eventually, he sees …; 8. Silas finds out that …;
9. Trying to reconstruct …; 10. Going through …; 11. He thinks back …;
12. We read about …; 13. Silas gets shaken …

Quotes: suggested solutions available via Augmented App. (1.6 Quotes)

Vocab & Language: These words are represented by the pictures: 1. roach end of joint/cigarette; 2. tire tracks; 3. scythe; 4. fishing rod; 5. filing cabinet; 6. shoe box; 7. pistol; 8. baseball glove; 9. coat and sneakers

1.7

This chapter focuses on: Larry

The story – Summary: To everybody's surprise and **amazement**, Cindy asks Larry out **on** a date. They want **to** go to a drive-in **movie**. Larry's classmates are totally **impressed** and Larry finally feels **accepted**. The date, however, turns **out** to be a mere **cover-up** for Cindy's plan to **meet** her real boyfriend. She **tells** Larry that she is **pregnant**. After he drops her **off** she is never seen **again**. Since he was the **one** to see her last, **Larry** finds himself accused of **abducting** and murdering her. Following **the** allegations against Larry, he **drops** out of high school, **joins** the army where he **trains** as a mechanic. His **father's** business gradually declines and **fails**, Carl eventually succumbs to **alcohol** and dies in a **car** accident. His mother Ina **withdraws** and eventually suffers from **dementia**. When his father dies, **Larry** returns to Chabot to **look** after Ina, but soon **has** to move her into a **nursing** home.

Quotes: suggested solutions available via Augmented App.
(1.7 Quotes – meaning)

Vocab & Language: C is for compliance, contraceptive, change, charm, cruelty…
D is for, dumb, dominant, doom, daddy, despair, defiance

1.8

This chapter focuses on: Silas

The story – Summary: Silas and **Angie** meet at a diner. He tells her about his friendship with "**scary Larry**" and adds the "**haunted house**" story as another social breaking point in Larry's life. Silas still hides the fact that it was him Cindy met that night after Larry dropped her off and his **regret** at not having said anything back then. He remembers how he once spent time at Larry's house and mowed the lawn with the **lawnmower**, which Larry was then **praised** for by his father Carl. **Chief French** believes that Larry's wounds are **self-inflicted**. Angie, however, disagrees. Silas meets **Wallace Stringfellow** and has an odd feeling about him. He then goes to the **cabin** on Larry's grounds and finds a **newly-dug grave** there.

7. Solutions of sorts

Quote: Abi-topic: Silas feels at home there because this place is one of the few constants in his life. Everything else always keeps changing. He belongs because he knows people and is liked by them, because he is familiar with places and life-stories and because the place holds happy memories of his childhood and his mother.

Quotes: suggested solutions available via Augmented App. (1.8 Quotes)

1.9

This chapter focuses on: Larry

The story – Summary: Summary available via Augmented App.
(1.9 Summary)

Quote: (223 10–15) In this passage, eating is likened to the basic human need of social interaction, human warmth and friendship. Somebody who is lonely (like Larry) will be able to go without food (or human warmth, affection and compassion) for a long time. After some time, they will no longer notice what they are missing, they've become numb even though they are suffering terribly from a lack of social interaction. When Wallace comes along (the foul bite because his friendship is not genuine), Larry realizes what he's been craving for. He once again starts to develop an appetite for life.

1.10

This chapter focuses on: Silas

The story – Summary: Silas has found **Tina Rutherford's body** in **Larry's cabin**. In hospital he tells Larry **not to confess**. Angie **can't understand why Silas never cleared Larry's name**.

Quotes: suggested solutions available via Augmented App.
(1.10 Quotes – meaning)

Vocab & Language: the words all describe **emotions or emotional states**

1.11

This chapter focuses on: Larry & Silas

The story – Summary: 1. "Stay with us, …; 2. "Did they find that girl?";
3. "It's amazing you're …; 4. "He saved your life…; 5. "Did you shoot …;
6. You had, if memory serves …; 7. "Can I talk …; 8. "We were friends," …;
9. "Okay. We all remember …; 10. smoked a little dope…;
11. "Maybe that's why you shot …; 12. "Do you think I …; 13. "Yeah. I do, Larry…

Quotes: suggested solutions available via Augmented App.
(1.11 Quotes – meaning)

1.12

This chapter focuses on: Larry & Silas

The story – Summary: Silas talks to Chief French about his date with Cindy
Walker. As a result of this "confession", he is taken off the case. Silas and Larry talk
about their relationship. Whereas Silas still finds it hard to call it a friendship,
Larry wants to apologize for what happened during the fight over the rifle. When
Silas meets Irina, she tells him about Wallace Stringfellow and the strange
abusive relationship he was having with her roommate Evelyn. The story of the
snake in the mailbox from the beginning of the book almost finds it conclusion,
and Silas is drawn in a more loyal and responsible light. Although he and Irina get
very drunk and she tries to seduce him, Silas doesn't cheat on Angie.

Quotes: suggested solutions available via Augmented App.
(1.12 Quotes – meaning)

1.13

This chapter focuses on: Larry

The story – Summary: During a thunderstorm, Larry remembers his childhood.
When they show the Rutherford case on TV and Larry's alleged involvement, he
realizes he must tell Chief French everything he remembers. Larry decides to take
his fate into his own hands from now on and wonders why he's always been a
victim.

Quotes: suggested solutions available via Augmented App.
(1.13 Quotes – meaning)

7. Solutions of sorts

1.14

This chapter focuses on: Silas

The story – Summary: Listen to a text summary via your Augmented App. (1.14 Summary – text)

Quotes – Silas and guilt: Silas realizes that he cannot "let himself off the hook" forever. He gets drunk in order to forget.

Foreshadowing: An experienced reader or someone who watches loads of films knows: The moment somebody says "Be careful!", something terrible is about to happen.

1.15

This chapter focuses on: Larry & Silas

The story – Summary: Listen to a text summary via your Augmented App. (1.15 Summary)

Suggested words for a wordle: French –Larry – Silas – Wallace – pitbull – mask – dead – incident – friend – lonesome – counseling – roommate

Quotes: suggested solutions available via Augmented App. (1.15 Quotes – meaning, 1.15 More quotes and 1.15 Quote – belonging)

1.16

This chapter focuses on: Larry & Silas

The story –Summary: Larry and Silas are in hospital together. Larry is finally cleared of the crimes and both French and Angie apologize for what he had to endure. Larry and Silas both realize they are half-brothers.

Quotes: suggested solutions available via Augmented App. (1.16 Quote – meaning)

1.17

This chapter focuses on: Larry & Silas

The story – Summary: Silas tries very hard to make up for his former wrongs, but Larry stubbornly refuses to talk to him.

Quotes: suggested solutions available via Augmented App.
(1.17 Quotes – meaning)

Vocab & Language – word field stubborn: words you might have added: bullheaded, hardened, unyielding, willful

1.18

This chapter focuses on: Larry & Silas

The story – Summary: Angie and Silas clean up Larry's house and set him up to become part of the community.

Quote: "a thing returned to its rightful place." (**314** 23). This phrase describes how after a very long time, the gun fits perfectly into the place it once occupied and once it is there, nobody can tell that it had been missing for so many years. If we take this to be symbolic, then it would suggest that by returning Larry's gun to its rightful place, Silas is also giving his own untroubled childhood hopes of a "world full of future and [sheer endless] possibility" back to Larry. Larry will hopefully be fully rehabilitated and included into the local community. He will find his own rightful place and this of course is the key to his gaining a feeling of 'belonging'.

1.19

This chapter focuses on: Larry & Silas

The story – Summary: Read this paragraph from back to front: When Larry leaves the hospital in the middle of the night to avoid the reporters, Silas finds him and gives him a lift home. As they drive past the Walker's old house, that by now is overgrown and barely visible, the reader is given a glimpse into their future. Some sense of normalcy is restored when the two men start talking about car engines and about Larry fixing Silas' car.

Quote: suggested solution available via Augmented App.
(1.19 Quote – meaning)

7. Solutions of sorts

2 Characters

Share and exchange information you've gathered with other students in your class to complete your character profiles.

3 Clues – Chapter by chapter

We're making access to the completed case-files just a wee bit tricky for you ;-) Check the Augmented downloads for clues… .

4 Classroom Material

These tasks will probably be done in class and your teacher has access to the solutions via the *Teacher's Guide* to the novel (Klett number 579901).

5 Digging Deeper

5.1 Quotes

Suggested solution available via Augmented App. (5.1 Quotes – meaning)

5.2 The story

The correct order of events, as mentioned in the novel:
1. We know Tina has disappeared … (**27** 9–11) – 2. Silas is about to discover … (**30** 15–16) – 3. Silas knows Larry. … (**30** 29-30) – 4. Silas recognizes the piece of clothing, … (**31** 16) – 5. Silas' girlfriend … (**35** 12–14) – 6. Silas and M&M go back … (**36** 20–21) – 7. He doesn't have a lot of … (**37** 30–32) – 8. People don't go … (**41** 15–16) – 9. Silas doesn't want to revive … (**43** 1-13) – 10. The locals all ostracize Larry… (**45** 18–19) – 11. Description of "white trash Avenue…" (**48** 14–18)

5.3 Quotes

They're either poor or new to the area. Larry is very observant. — **56** 1

58 1–2 — Larry feels uncomfortable around black kids.

He notices how his mother's mood changes. He realizes he shouldn't have told her. — **59** 13–14

67 4–7 — Larry observes Carl and his admiring friends. He's not part of the crowd.

Detailed description of how he watches (almost stalks) Cindy. — **68** 8ff.

71 25–27 — Larry realizes that David and Ken are up to something but he's desperate to be accepted.

Larry had hoped that he would be accepted and get more support from the white kids, but they still laugh at him. — **75** 5–9

78 4–8 — A subtle hint that maybe Carl gave Alice a car since he can no longer give them a lift after Ina's intervention.

Larry is kind and caring. He'd do anything for this friendship. — **81** 5–8

7. Solutions of sorts

5.4 Clues & Quotes

Clues

Stephen King books: Larry still loves horror. Does he just like reading it?
Is he capable of committing a crime?
Unreturned phone call: Is Silas hiding something? Is he involved in the crime?
Why is he avoiding Larry? Is he guilty of something?

Quotes

Suggested solution available via Augmented App. (5.4 Quotes – meaning)

5.5 Quotes

98 5–6	Ina cares a lot for Larry. Larry isn't very healthy.
99 21–22	Carl is a heavy drinker.
100 12–15	Larry secretly thinks about the strange relationship between his dad and Silas' mum.
101 9–10	Silas doesn't like snakes.
102 7–8	Alice doesn't want her son to befriend Larry. Larry thinks it's a question of race, but the true reason is revealed later.
106 9–10	Cecil is mean and dangerous.
111 5–11	Silas is critical of Larry's passiveness.
113 12–13	Ina has had enough.
116 33–34	Carl hates it when Larry reads too much.

5.7 Quotes

Suggested solution available via Augmented App. (5.7 Quotes – meaning)

5.9 Friendship

Suggested solution available via Augmented App.
(5.9 Friendship)

5.11 Post-reading

How do Chief French and Sheriff Lolly try to get a confession out of Larry.

First, French tries to lighten the mood and be sympathetic by expressing that he knows what it feels like to be in hospital. (p. 254) Then they follow a bit of a "good cop – bad cop" routine and very directly ask Larry whether he shot himself and whether he raped and killed the Rutherford girl. (p. 256). On a second visit the Sheriff who worked the Walker case shows sympathy by releasing Larry's restraints and talking about the past and about how there was never any evidence to support Larry's involvement in the Walker crime, even though he had no alibi. Then French picks up again and suggest that these old stories and the loneliness they caused may have made Larry to abduct Tina Rutherford. The way French describes what might have happened and that the community was partly responsible as well as the way 'modern' girls dress and behave (very sexist description, by the way) is designed to lure Larry into admitting that he committed a crime and then attempted suicide out of shame or regret. Seeing as Larry has lost parts of his memory, he is quite vulnerable and potentially easy to manipulate. French permanently tries to give an understanding impression as if Larry hadn't really done anything evil.

5.15 Quotes

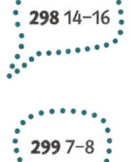

298 14–16

This scene is **symbolic**: Larry doesn't want the mask any longer. It is the mask that links him to his former life but never helped in getting him accepted. On the contrary, he almost got killed.

299 7–8

This can be seen as an attempt at **humor** or **comic relief**.

7. Solutions of sorts

5.16 Language in use

Story anchor woman: She reports on the lead "story of local violence and justice". While Constable Jones was investigating the snake-in-mailbox case, he came across an entire snake den. The owner, Wallace Stringfellow, when questioned set his dog on Jones. The officer was injured and only found because a Town Hall employee couldn't contact him and called back-up. When followed by the police officers, Stringfellow escaped into the woods and took his own life.
The unexpected turn in this story is the evidence that showed up in Stringfellow's house that links him not only to the drug dealer M&M, but also to the disappearance of Tina Rutherford. The police are unwilling to comment at this stage.

As a **stylistic device** the neutral report delivered by the late news anchor woman serves to unemotionally reveal solutions to at least two of the four crimes. It is deliberately set apart from the emotional part of the story dealing with Larry's and Silas' relationship.

5.17 Comic relief

Some examples of humor and / or comic relief are:

(**82** 20–22) "See you tonight at the Bus?" "Might be hard." "Damn, I hope so." (Play on words – where Silas means it might be difficult for him to make it, Angie interprets it as him being sexually aroused.)

(**88** 32–33) "Shit," he said, laughing. The chickens agreed. (Silas expects to find a potentially dangerous person, yet only comes across the chickens, who are just as scared by his shot as he was by their movement moments earlier.)

(**181** 27–28) "Are you family?" he asked, then gave a half smile to let Silas know he didn't have to answer, it was a joke. (Asking an Afro-American man whether he's related to a white patient seems stupid. Of course this later turns out to be true because they are half-brothers, i.e. Silas actually is 'Family'.)

(**299** 6–8) "You got a strange taste in friends." "I don't know if you noticed," Larry said, "but I ain't had a lot of options." (With nobody wanting to be your friend, you take what comes along, even if they're 'strange'.)

5.18 The story

Cleaning Larry's house means that not just the signs of the current crime are being removed, but maybe that Larry's slate is being cleaned, his name is cleared. He is innocent (has been all along) and can now start a new life. It is also an act of making amends, of trying to make something right. It stands for the idea of a clean break with the past and a new beginning.

5.19 Setting

The passage (**319** 30 – **320** 2) tells you the following things about Fulsom:

- The place is dying
- The streets are quiet and deserted
- Shops have closed down
- Only a few have been able to change and adapt to a different trade (tanning/pedicure)
- The box of chicken must come from a fast-food joint, someone driving past must have thrown the remains out of their car window
- In numerous other passages, the desolation is described in similar terms (pp. 38/39, ll. 20 ff.)

Credits

Photo Credits

45, 160.6 Shutterstock (sirtravelalot), New York; **50, 161.1** Shutterstock (Everett Collection), New York; **45,161.7** Shutterstock (Visionsi), New York; **51, 161** Shutterstock (Sabphoto), New York; **48.1** Shutterstock (Isabel Eve), New York; **48.2** Shutterstock (vsl), New York; **48.3** Shutterstock (Serz_72), New York; **48.4** Shutterstock (Pranch), New York; **48.5** Shutterstock (Deyan Georgiev), New York; **48.6** Shutterstock (AlexLMX), New York; **48.7** Shutterstock (AVA Bitter), New York; **48.8** Shutterstock (deepspacedave), New York; **48.9** Shutterstock (Burbelo), New York; **160.1** Shutterstock (perm), New York; **160.2** Shutterstock (Everett Historical), New York; **160.3** Shutterstock (Jason Stitt), New York; **160.4** Shutterstock (Kristina Konovalova), New York; **160.5** picture alliance/AP Images; **160.7** Shutterstock (Alan Poulson Photography), New York; **160.8** Shutterstock (John Wollwerth), New York; **160.8** Shutterstock (mangostock), New York; **160.9** Bigstock (Martinan), New York, NY; **161.10** Shutterstock (Raihana Asral), New York; **161.12** Bigstock (alexeys), New York, NY; **161.13** Shutterstock (De Visu), New York; **161.14** Bigstock (makam69), New York, NY; **161.15** Shutterstock (Andrey_Popov), New York; **161.2** Shutterstock (Nataly Reinch), New York; **161.3** Shutterstock (Emma manners), New York; **161.4** Shutterstock (Mindmo), New York; **161.5** Shutterstock (Benoit Daoust), New York; **161.6** Shutterstock (J.D.S), New York; **161.8** Shutterstock (Sabphoto), New York; **161.9** Shutterstock (kml), New York; **170** Shutterstock (anpannan), New York

Music Credits

You have access to the following three music tracks via the Augmented App.

- page 45: Track 06 from *Driving Miss Daisy* (Original Soundtrack); Music Composed, Arranged and Performed by Hans Zimmer © 1989, Warner Brothers Inc
- page 51: *Stayin' Alive* by the Bee Gees © 1977 (This version from the Album *The Ultimate Bee Gees*.)
- page 170: *Hazard* by Richard Marx © 1991 (This version from the Album *Greatest Hits*.)